REFLECTIONS
FOR BUSY
EDUCATORS

REFLECTIONS FOR BUSY EDUCATORS

180 Affirmations to Help You Through the School Year

Jo Ann Lordahl

CORWIN PRESS, INC.
A Sage Publications Company
Thousand Oaks, California

Excerpts from *Paradigms* by Joel Barker, copyright © 1992 by Joel Barker. Reprinted by permission of author.

Excerpts from *Miss Giardino* by Dorothy Bryant, copyright © 1978 by Dorothy Bryant. Reprinted by permission of author. Dorothy Bryant's 10 novels also include *Ella Price's Journal* and *The Kin of Ata*. All are available at bookstores or from Ata Books, 1928 Stuart St., Berkeley, CA 94703, (510) 841-9613.

Days 46 and 60 are excerpted from *Money Meditations for Women,* copyright © 1994 by Jo Ann Lordahl. Reprinted by permission of Celestial Arts, Berkeley, CA.

"The Escapee" by Gail White was first published in *Calyx: A Journal of Art and Literature by Women,* vol. 15:3, Fall/Winter 1994/1995. Reprinted with permission of the publisher and the author. Copyright © 1994 Gail White.

For information address:

Corwin Press, Inc.
A Sage Publications Company
2455 Teller Road
Thousand Oaks, California 91320
e-mail: order@corwin.sagepub.com

SAGE Publications Ltd.
6 Bonhill Street
London EC2A 4PU
United Kingdom

SAGE Publications India Pvt. Ltd.
M-32 Market
Greater Kailash I
New Delhi 110 048 India

Printed in the United States of America

Library of Congress Cataloging-in-Publication Data

Lordahl, Jo Ann.
    Reflections for busy educators : 180 affirmations to help you
through the school year / Jo Ann Lordahl.
        p.   cm.
    Includes bibliographical references.
    ISBN 0-8039-6376-9 (cloth). — ISBN 0-8039-6320-3 (pbk.)
        1. Education—Quotations, maxims, etc. 2. Quotations, English.
    I. Title.
    PN6084.E38L67   1995
    370—dc20   95-21433

This book is printed on acid-free paper.

95 96 97 98 99 10 9 8 7 6 5 4 3 2 1

Corwin Press Production Editor: S. Marlene Head

ABOUT THE AUTHOR

Jo Ann Lordahl is a writer, therapist, workshop leader, and speaker. She has held jobs as diverse as director of psychological services for students at Florida Atlantic University to teaching applied psychology at Brock University in Canada, and from managing the Task Force Division for Statistical Tabulating Corporation in St. Louis to teaching statistics at Florida A&M University.

She has also taught community education courses, diet workshops, poetry-as-therapy workshops, money and spirituality workshops, and writing and journal-keeping workshops, and she has coordinated Women's Voices, a performance-based poetry group in Gainesville, Florida.

Lordahl is the author of *Money Meditations for Women* (1994), *Reconnecting the Healing Circle* (1993), *The End of Motherhood: New Identities, New Lives* (1990), and *Those Subtle Weeds*, a Florida romance published in 1974. She also has published six volumes of poetry, and her work has appeared in small-press publications, including *Negative Capability, Piddiddle, Impetus, Skylight, The Communicator,* and *Woodrider.* Her lyric play, *Four Women Speak,* was last performed in 1994 at Women in Religion in Miami, Florida.

Lordahl lives in the Marietta T. Nichols house in the historic district of Gainesville and enjoys fixing up old houses for fun and profit. She feels that working with her hands is the perfect antidote for the many speeches and workshops she gives, and she loves coming home to the quiet peacefulness of her house and seeing her two granddaughters, Jessa and Leah, who live around the corner.

For information on her workshops and speeches, write or call Jo Ann Lordahl, P.O. Box 2666, Gainesville, FL 32602, 904-376-2807 (phone and FAX).

INTRODUCTION

Reflections for Busy Educators offers encouragement and strength as you begin each day as an educator. This book also helps your search for personal growth. Some pages will explore heart, soul, and spirituality—meaning that common core of human experience that shines true across religions, times, and cultures. Along with a search for meaning, you will also find a few practical hints, some laughter, and numerous words to inspire you.

"Three of the key elements in the art of working together are how to deal with change, how to deal with conflict, and how to reach our potential," says Max De Pree in *Leadership Is an Art*. As you explore themes in this book, you will be surprised with contrasts and paradoxes. You will gain new ideas for dealing with change, conflict, and reaching your potential, and also for helping others.

Reflections for Busy Educators saves you time by consolidating resources and ideas. For your convenience, a complete list of references, as well as a short list of books to help you explore more, appears at the end of the text. Remember, this book doesn't care if you write in it, turn down its pages, or loan it to a friend, parent, or colleague. You can even give it to your boss (who no doubt needs it!).

We know the difficulties we face in education stem from problems in our society. But we don't know what to do about them. Take this opportunity to explore the insights offered from significant books, from my own experiences, and from my friends and colleagues. Use these themes and ideas as points for your exploration. Your own deepest longings will trigger needed change. Heart, hope, and faith can supply the strength we need to do our jobs in uncommon and newly satisfying ways.

The word *crisis*, when written in Chinese, is composed of two characters. One means danger and the other, opportunity. We do indeed live in perilous times. But perilous times can offer us our greatest opportunities. Together our possibilities have no end; united we can do what we want. We can energize our schools and change our lives.

DAY 1

A great Master must also be a great teacher. . . . Had he begun the lessons with breathing exercises, he would never have been able to convince you that you owe them anything decisive. You had to suffer shipwreck through your own efforts before you were ready to seize the life belt he threw you. Believe me, I know from my own experience that the Master knows you and each of his pupils much better than we know ourselves. He reads in the souls of his pupils more than they care to admit.

EUGEN HERRIGE

It's always a question, isn't it—what we will do with our knowledge of others, with what we read from their souls and daily behavior.

AFFIRMATION

Making full use of my art, information, and experience, I am a great teacher.

DAY 2

I have been continually astonished to discover just how intricately children come to examine the social system, the political and economic facts of life in our society. I had always imagined myself rather sensible and untouched by those romantic nineteenth-century notions of childhood "innocence." As a child psychiatrist I had even committed myself to a professional life based on the faith that young children see and feel what is happening in their family life. . . . Yet I had never quite realized that children so quickly learn to estimate who can vote, or who has the money to frequent this kind of restaurant or that kind of theater, or what groups of people contribute to our police force—and why.

ROBERT COLES

AFFIRMATION

I never underestimate the intelligence and sensitivity of children and young adults. Or how they will be affected by the situations around them.

DAY 3

It's all lies you know, about childhood
being so happy. I've been a sojourner
in that country. The short people have no power.
Money and love are rationed to them
by the tall gods. Their diet is daily
humiliation. I escaped by the hardest,
scrambling over rocks, falling down cliffs
when I had to, trusting to hit
water at the bottom. I never looked back
and have tried to forget the worst, except in dreams.
My advice to my sisters and brothers still in bonds
is to get tall fast.

"The Escapee," Gail White

It's probably our job to help others "get tall fast." We'll surely do better if we remember being short.

AFFIRMATION

I am excellent at helping myself and others "grow taller."

DAY 4

"Oh, Miss Giardino, can't I have one more day to finish? I know I was late last time too, but I . . ."

"But, Miss Giardino, I get A's in all my other classes. I never got a C on a paper before. My aunt used to teach English and she thought it was good!"

"Can't I make it up? No, I wouldn't call it cheating. Me, copy? No, I don't want to see your copy of the essay in the book. Oh, Miss Giardino, you can't flunk me and ruin my life!"

"Miss Giardino, you're so mean!"

"Miss Giardino, you a racist!"

Dorothy Bryant

Is there a teacher alive who hasn't heard some versions of these remarks? And who doesn't sigh in their soul when they have to deal with them one more time?

AFFIRMATION

I develop safe and sane ways to deal with the inevitable excuses.

DAY 5

He said, "Well, the reason I'm giving him Ds [instead of Fs] is because I'm fully convinced that he'll catch on to this very soon and when he does, I'm sure his grades will come right on up." He said, "I don't want to start giving him grades now which would impact his getting into college."

Isn't that neat? So, by golly, in about the third or fourth month, suddenly the light came on and I really caught on to the logic of plane geometry. The net result of that was I got 100s in my midterm examination, so this guy kept me alive.

AN ADULT REMEMBERING A TEACHER
(QUOTED IN BLUMBERG AND BLUMBERG)

It's all in the skill and experience. Yet mostly the path to experience leads through the jungle of mistakes.

AFFIRMATION

I am not afraid to gain the experience I need.

DAY 6

The spider dances her web without knowing that there are flies who will get caught in it. The fly, dancing nonchalantly on a sunbeam, gets caught in the net without knowing what lies in store. But through both of them "It" dances, and inside and outside reunite in this dance. So, too, the archer hits the target without having aimed—more I cannot say.

EUGEN HERRIGE

The great educator is a great dreamer and shaper. Lives flow through our lives and ourselves. We work on trust, never asking for a finished product—only improvement.

AFFIRMATION

I am grateful for each day and person, and when the time comes to let them go, I let them go.

DAY 7

We can't change the past, but we can learn from it and build on it.

We can't control the future, but we can shape it and enhance the possibilities for our children and grandchildren.

We can't discern in the present the fullness of our actions and their impact, but we can be pioneers in our time, exploring fully the crevices and cracks where knowledge and new insights might be found.

We can explore our spectrum of relationships and confront our complacency and certainty about the way things are.

ERROLD D. COLLYMORE
(IN MORRISON-REED AND JAMES)

A world where 19 million U.S. children live in a home with no father, where 71% of U.S. adults are overweight, and where heartland Oklahoma City is hit with a terrorist bomb—this is not the world that we grew up in.

AFFIRMATION

I am a pioneer.
I know that change is necessary.

DAY 8

I do not happen to be a believer in the cliche that "Virtue is its own reward." As far as I'm concerned, the reward for virtue should be at least a chocolate sundae, and preferably a cruise to the Bahamas. Virtue is damned hard work and frequently uncomfortable.

BARBARA SHER

I once had a character say in an unpublished novel, "If no one else gives me value, then I give it to myself." Many times we don't think about giving to ourselves. But we're the closest person around and we know exactly what we want and need!

AFFIRMATION

If no one else gives me rewards, I give them to myself.

DAY 9

Be a facilitator, not a dictator. If it is your idea, they may have no incentive to see it work. After all, it will be your idea that fails, not theirs.

The best encouragement is when we are supporting other people's ideas, goals, and beliefs about themselves, not when we are "telling" them what we expect.

CONNIE PODESTA

Because it's so much easier to tell rather than show and to tell rather than *be* by example, getting trapped in this telling, talking, and lecturing space is easy. Instead of confrontation or criticism, M. Scott Peck in *The Road Less Traveled* shares an intriguing list of how to bring about changes we want: "by example, suggestion, parable, reward and punishment, questioning, prohibition or permission, creation of experiences, organizing with others, and so on."

AFFIRMATION

I love helping others by helping them to help themselves.

DAY 10

A good archer can shoot further with a medium-strong bow than an un-spiritual archer can with the strongest. It does not depend on the bow, but on the presence of mind, on the vitality and awareness with which you shoot. In order to unleash the full force of [your] spiritual awareness, you must perform the ceremony differently: rather as a good dancer dances. If you do this, your movements will spring from the center, from the seat of right breathing.

EUGEN HERRIGE

This is the practical side of the spiritual—that the spiritual deepens our very selves so that we are more. We can do more and do it more effectively.

AFFIRMATION

I cultivate my spiritual awareness.

DAY 11

Some days you need tools. Some days you need weapons. You need your sense of humor every day.

MELODIE CHENEVERT

Every day is another chance to begin anew. Or to improve the life you have. It's a time to bring balance and play, commitment and joy into deeper alliance.

AFFIRMATION

Through planning and choice I create the life I want.

DAY 12

Life in the late twentieth century creates many obstacles for all of us when we seek our spiritual center. An entrenched pragmatic orientation places a premium on technical logic. A widespread tendency to specialize and compartmentalize leads us to dichotomize work and play, male and female, career and family, thinking and feeling, reason and spirit. We relegate spirituality to churches, temples, and mosques—for those who still attend them. We shun it at work. . . . The message warns against trying to put someone else in charge of your spiritual journey. Instead, recognize and trust the power within you.

LEE G. BOLMAN AND TERRENCE E. DEAL

"It does not matter how long your spirit lies dormant and unused. One day you hear a song, look at an object, or see a vision, and you feel its presence. It can't be bought, traded, or annihilated, because its power comes from its story. No one can steal your spirit. You have to give it away. You can also take it back," says Carl Hammerschlag in *The Theft of the Spirit.*

AFFIRMATION

I search for spirit and soul.

DAY 13

Native people believed the best teaching came from example. What I've tried to show in my life and in this book are:

1. *Don't be afraid of your feelings, and don't be ashamed to admit you have them.*
2. *Speak your truth firmly and clearly.*
3. *Find your path and purpose and follow it.*
4. *Respect the visions of others.*
5. *Get involved.*

WABUN WIND

W hat do you try to show in your life? What are your prescriptions for being a good teacher of others?

AFFIRMATION

More and more, I become the person I want to be.
More and more, I am a role model for others.

DAY 14

A lot of the kids we're seeing now aren't immoral; they're amoral. They just haven't learned. Their biggest source of interaction has been with something you plug in and turn on.

PHYLLIS SMITH-HANSEN
(QUOTED IN LICKONA)

P araphrasing Mother Jones's "Pray for the dead and fight like hell for the living," I pray for the wonderful past and fight like hell for the kids of the not-so-wonderful present. For inspiration and fun, you'll enjoy reading the book this quotation came from, *Wild Women: Crusaders, Curmudgeons, and Completely Corsetless Ladies in the Otherwise Virtuous Victorian Era* by Autumn Stephens.

AFFIRMATION

I fight for better lives.

DAY 15

I have come to a frightening conclusion that I am the decisive element in the classroom. . . . As a teacher, I possess tremendous power to make a child's life miserable or joyous. I can be a tool of torture or an instrument of inspiration. I can humiliate or humor, hurt or heal. In all situations, it is my response that decides whether a crisis will be escalated or de-escalated, and a child humanized or dehumanized.

HAIM GINOTT

The simplest things can be the hardest to do and the most powerful. I act from my heart, which is constantly growing.

AFFIRMATION

With courage and grace, I accept my responsibilities.

DAY 16

I was in the first grade when this happened. We had a girl in our class named Barbara who used to get out of her seat all the time and this irritated Mrs. Wyman, my teacher. So Mrs. Wyman tied Barbara into her chair and Barbara wet her pants. I was so embarrassed for her and felt so badly for her. Then I remembered that I was talking to myself in my head and I thought, "Do all the other boys and girls talk to themselves in their head?" I think that was the first time I was aware of thinking, the thought process. And it was the first time I was aware of thinking about thinking.

MEMORIES OF SCHOOL
(QUOTED IN BLUMBERG AND BLUMBERG)

AFFIRMATION

Every day my consciousness grows, along with my power to effect positive change.

DAY 17

Good listeners do not turn on and off at will, shutting out what they think they do or do not want to hear. They consider this kind of voluntary deafness a high-risk activity that leads to missing not only important surface information but also the inner meaning of what is going on. . . . Listening itself is worth the effort, that there will, in fact, be time to take care of all the other pressing concerns. It is, ultimately, the gift of ourselves and our time, in unselfish service to someone else.

KATHARINE LE MEÉ

AFFIRMATION

I am a good listener.
I practice being a good listener.

DAY 18

There is no one but us. There is no one to send, nor a clean hand, nor a pure heart on the face of the earth, nor in the earth, but only us, a generation comforting ourselves with the notion that we have come at an awkward time, that our innocent fathers are all dead—as if innocence had ever been—and our children busy and troubled, and we ourselves unfit, not yet ready, having each of us chosen wrongly, made a false start, failed, yielded to impulse and the tangled comfort of pleasures, and grown exhausted, unable to seek the thread, weak, and involved. But there is no one but us. There never has been.

ANNIE DILLARD
(QUOTED IN SEWELL)

What gives meaning to life is being connected to something beyond our own ego, says James W. Jones in *In the Middle of This Road We Call Our Life*. This meaning is "an essentially spiritual experience."

AFFIRMATION

I accept the work that I must do.

DAY 19

What exists within an acorn must contain all the vital elements for the development of a tree. Nourishment from earth, water, bacteria, energy from the sun, oxygen from the air, etc., are all required for the fulfillment of its potential. Accidents can permanently deform or kill it, but the things most essential to its development must be within.

DAVID M. MORIARTY

The child is father and mother to the man and the woman. Each human being that I encounter has her or his own destiny. How scary and how miraculous.

AFFIRMATION

I am mindful of each life I encounter.

DAY 20

"I am too old a soldier to mount an unnecessary charge."
"Quite," she agreed. "And I have cleared up after too many."

ANNE PERRY

This is precisely why we must know ourselves and prioritize our desires. Mounting unnecessary charges wastes precious time and energy.

Cleaning up after other people's messes, and our own, is a true pain. We must learn not to make the messes, physical or emotional. (And the sooner the better.) Sometimes I deliberately use this pain of cleaning up old confusion (unsorted writing, the garden's disaster) as a lesson to do better next time, reminding myself that organizing as I go along is much easier and that decisions deferred can quickly become more trouble than they're worth.

Looking at priority lists helps me. George Abbott, the playwright who died at age 107, made a priority list as a young man. When asked in an interview at 102 if his list was still valid, he replied *yes*. His priority list: Health. Work. Love. Play.

AFFIRMATION

I know my values, and my priority list suits me.

DAY 21

*The pride to which we aspire is not in being men but in being men who . . .
are living their lives in a way that will make a difference.*

*We must be transformers of selfhood—our own and others'. If we do not,
we will have betrayed women's lives utterly, and we will have lost a part of
ourselves that is precious and rare on this earth.*

JOHN STOLTENBERG

A male friend used to mutter, "Why me? Life went along the
same for hundreds of years. Thousands. Generations of men ruled the
roost. And now I've got to change and become equal!"

But he spoke with a twinkle and from his place in the forefront of
change.

AFFIRMATION

I am a leader and innovator of necessary change.

DAY 22

*If we all refuse to serve, until we attain perfection, there will be no service.
The fact is that perfection is attained through service.*

MAHATMA GANDHI
(QUOTED IN NAIR)

A woman brought her daughter to Gandhi. The woman
asked Gandhi to tell her daughter not to eat sugar. Gandhi thought
for a moment and then asked the woman to return in two weeks. Two
weeks later, Gandhi told the daughter not to eat sugar. Surprised, the
woman asked Gandhi, "Why didn't you tell her that two weeks ago?"

Gandhi replied, "Two weeks ago I was still eating sugar."

AFFIRMATION

My life is my message.

DAY 23

If you don't know where you are going, you will probably end up someplace else.

LAURENCE J. PETER

Do you have a goal list? If you don't, this is the day to begin one. It's easy. Grab paper and pen, find a quiet place, and prepare to dream. And write. And write. First, give yourself unlimited time, talent, money, supportive relations and friends, and don't stop until you have a 100-item wish list. Now choose one or more to put on the front burner and start to work!

AFFIRMATION

I know where I am going and how I will get there.

DAY 24

I am appalled, yet I understand. After five years of teaching I sense something happening to me, a kind of erosion, wave after wave of students washing over me, wearing me down. Last summer did not seem long enough. The usual recovery, the eagerness to return, did not come in September. The other teachers tell me I work too hard, must learn to "pace myself," must "develop outside interests." What they mean is that I must learn to hold back, give less of myself, care less, blunt all the edges, the feeling edges that have grown so worn and raw from being rubbed against by so many young people who need so much.

DOROTHY BRYANT

Remember the lifeboat story—that if we take too many into the lifeboat of our lives all hands will sink, including us.

AFFIRMATION

I find healthy and realistic balances between my needs and the needs of others.

DAY 25

*I care. I care about it all. It takes too much energy not to care. Yesterday I counted twenty-six gray hairs on the top of my head all from trying **not** to care. . . . The **why** of why we are here is an intrigue for adolescents; the **how** is what must command the living. Which is why I have lately become an insurgent again.*

LORRAINE HANSBERRY

AFFIRMATION

On better days I am an insurgent for education.

DAY 26

The old rules were simple: States and localities paid schools to teach students until they were eighteen or nineteen years of age. After that, the per-student payment disappeared. Clear boundaries. But now, the United States is facing up to the fact that many of our "graduated" students cannot read, write, or compute. The value of their high school diploma, in the real world of competition, is zero. . . .

To compete with the world in the twenty-first century, the United States cannot afford to have anything less than competence. The new rules are being written even as you read this.

JOEL ARTHUR BARKER

Learning used to be a rote activity, a transfer of information. "The new paradigm views learning as the development of increasingly sophisticated judgment and skills across a spectrum of integrated disciplines," says Kenneth Wilson in *Redesigning Education.* Mastery is demonstrated by performance.

AFFIRMATION

I keep my mind on—and develop for myself and others—mastery, performance, and competency.

DAY 27

Being an artist means, not reckoning and counting, but ripening like the tree which does not force its sap and stands confident in the storms of spring without the fear that after them may come no summer. It does come. But it comes only to the patient, who are there as though eternity lay before them, so unconcernedly still and wide. I learn it daily, learn it with pain to which I am grateful: patience is everything!

RAINER MARIA RILKE

Replace "artist" with "teacher" in the above quote and we go to the heart of our task in teaching.

AFFIRMATION

I ponder patience, and how I can use its strength.

DAY 28

With caring the concept of work changes fundamentally. Caring is reflected directly in your day-to-day behavior. And from that caring comes great enthusiasm and commitment, which leads in a wonderful feedback loop to even greater productivity, innovation, and self-initiation.

JOEL ARTHUR BARKER

AFFIRMATION

I follow my heart to find out where my caring is and how I can further it.

DAY 29

I'm convinced that Arthur Jones could have been anything he wanted to be. He could have been president . . . yet Jonesy had decided to spend this incarnation teaching band at Lawrence High School. He was one of the acknowledged princes of the school, a position he could have held solely on strength of personality. But it also didn't hurt that for four years he had produced the number one school band in the state of New York.

MICKEY HART

"All of us have unfulfilled dreams, wounds that need to be healed, old business that seeks resolution," says Carl Hammerschlag in *The Theft of the Spirit.* "We simply don't create the 'field of dreams' necessary to allow that to happen. It's not because we don't want to, it's because we don't believe."

AFFIRMATION

I find my place and I shine there.
I enjoy learning from excellent teachers.

DAY 30

Most of us miss out on life's big prizes. The Pulitzer. The Nobel. Oscars. Tonys. Emmys. But we're all eligible for life's small pleasures. A pat on the back. A kiss behind the ear. A four-pound bass. A full moon. An empty parking space. A crackling fire. A great meal. A glorious sunset. Hot soup. Cold beer. Don't fret about copping life's grand awards. Enjoy its tiny delights. There are plenty for all of us.

UNITED TECHNOLOGIES CORPORATION
(QUOTED IN *QUOTATIONS TO CHEER YOU UP*)

AFFIRMATION

Today I mentally say, "Thank you," to the universe for every nice thing that happens to me.

DAY 31

A business is what you make it, she said calmly. If you believe it's a machine, it will be. A temple? It can be that too. Spirit and faith are the core of human life. Without them, you lose your way. You live without zest. You go through the motions, but there's no passion . . .

Look, I'm running an organization, not a church . . .

What do you hope to run it with? More sweat? More control? More tricks and gimmicks?

Maybe some wisdom. He hadn't meant to say that, but it came out anyway.

Wisdom comes later. First you have to look into your heart . . .

I can't tell you what's in your heart. . . . Only you really know what's in your heart.

LEE G. BOLMAN AND TERRENCE E. DEAL

Education is what we make it. We can make it what we want it to be.

AFFIRMATION

I search my heart for its joy and passion and wisdom.

DAY 32

Thirty years of research show that 90 percent of achievement in school is determined by how much TV a child watches, school attendance, and how much reading is done at home. Studies also repeatedly show that parental involvement is more important to academic success than the family's income level.

LYRIC WALLWORK WINIK

AFFIRMATION

I keep up with research, incorporate it into my work, and perhaps even contact parents and encourage their involvement.

DAY 33

More teachers would, I believe, assign more homework if they knew what the research shows.

When low-ability students do just one to three hours of homework a week, their grades are usually as high as those of average-ability students who do no homework.

When average-ability students do three to five hours of homework a week, their grades usually equal those of high-ability students who do no homework.

THOMAS LICKONA

AFFIRMATION

I get the information, training, and help I need to do an outstanding job.

DAY 34

The teachers arrived, gray-haired and jolly. . . . One was tall and stout, the other small and spare. They were both classic examples of a dying breed, the spinster schoolteacher who had given her life to education. The world was not going to be the same without their dedication.

MARY DAHEIM

It may be, like the monks and nuns, celibates and renunciates of old, that too few are carrying too heavy a load. And that now we'll all have to pitch in and do our part to discover what education really is and how best to support it.

AFFIRMATION

I am proud to be an educator.

DAY 35

There are some who hunger and thirst after whatever it is they haven't seen and smelt, and those are the ones who sit like this, one leg wrapped twice around the other under a skirt smutcht [an old form of the word smudged—dirtied or stained] with the palm sweat of effort, frowning into the black figures of the text with infinite patience and desire . . . whose best hope of life here would be marriage to a ham-handed and imperious laborer chosen from a radius of no more than thirty miles; six children in a decade; varicose veins; the loss of her teeth, her figure, and if she was unlucky, the job she grew to despise with the passing years.

JANET BURROWAY

AFFIRMATION

Ignorance is the monster. I like to kill monsters.

DAY 36

All work is creative work if done by a thinking mind, and no work is creative if done by a blank who repeats in uncritical stupor a routine he [or she] has learned from others.

AYN RAND

Or as Carl Hammerschlag says in *The Theft of the Spirit*: "Don't identify too strongly with what you now know; that 'truth' is impermanent. Identify with the possibility that at every moment you can emerge from your blind self to see in the dark."

AFFIRMATION

I bring my thinking mind to my work and my life.

Both men belonged to the great body of psychologically misshapen people that I refer to as The Pool. Members of The Pool leave behind warehouses of official paperwork as evidence that they have occupied the planet for a certain period of time. Their names are entered early on in welfare case histories, child-abuse investigations, clinic admissions for rat bites and malnutrition. Later on these same people provide jobs for an army of truant officers, psychologists, public defenders, juvenile probation officers, ambulance attendants, emergency-room personnel, street cops, prosecutors, jailers, prison guards, alcohol- and drug-treatment counselors, bail bondsmen, adult parole authorities, and the county morticians who put the final punctuation mark in their files.

The irony is that without The Pool we would probably have to justify our jobs by refocusing our attention and turning the key on slumlords, industrial polluters, and the coalition of defense contractors and militarists who look upon the national treasury as a personal slush fund.

JAMES LEE BURKE

"If you think education is expensive—try ignorance," say the bumper stickers attributed to Derek Bok.

"It is no use saying 'we are doing our best.' You have got to succeed in doing what is necessary," as Winston Churchill said about winning World War II.

AFFIRMATION

I carefully choose where to place my energy and efforts.
I support the power of early intervention.

DAY 38

Take risks: if you win, you will be happy; if you lose you will be wise.

Think back over risks you have taken and those you have refused. Think of things you wanted and which you would not take, even small ones.

Not hanging in my closet is that gorgeous frivolous red dress I was too cowardly at twenty to buy. Or did a part of me know I lacked the nerve to wear it? If I'd bought the red dress, it would be long-ago history. Now it hangs in my closet of memory as a reminder.

AFFIRMATION

I take appropriate risks.

DAY 39

The teaching of the rules of the stroke economy to children constitutes the basic training for Lovelessness. As in all scripting, Lovelessness is based on injunctions and attributions.

The injunctions of the stroke economy are:

1. *Don't give strokes if you have them to give.*
2. *Don't ask for strokes when you need them.*
3. *Don't accept strokes if you want them.*
4. *Don't reject strokes when you don't want them.*
5. *Don't give yourself strokes.*

AFFIRMATION

I know about "scripts" and I help myself and others to transcend them.

DAY 40

The only good is knowledge, and the only evil is ignorance.

SOCRATES
(QUOTED IN SELDES)

"Speech is civilization itself," says Thomas Mann, adding that "the word—even the most contradictory word—preserves contact. It is silence which isolates."

A long overdue insight for me is that no response *is* a response. My tendency has been to reach out and when the other retreats or isn't there, then I reach further and still further. I've mistakenly tried to carry both sides of a relationship.

Now, when I receive "no response," I'm learning to look for more responsive people!

AFFIRMATION

I have the people I need (and who need me) for contact, friendship, community, relationship, intimacy, and love.

DAY 41

*She unlocks her office door, then locks it behind her to disguise the fact that she's in there. It's not her office hours but the students take advantage. They can smell her out, like sniffer dogs; they'll seize any opportunity to suck up to her or whine, or attempt to impress her, or foist upon her their versions of sulky defiance. **I'm just a human being,** Tony wants to say to them. But of course she isn't. She's a human being with power. There isn't much of it, but it's power all the same.*

MARGARET ATWOOD

AFFIRMATION

I employ power with wit and wisdom.

DAY 42

In spite of the successes achieved by the women's movement, the prevailing myth in our culture is that certain people, positions, and events have more inherent value than others. These people, positions, and events are usually masculine or male-defined. Male norms have become the social standard for leadership, personal autonomy, and success in this culture, and in comparison women find themselves perceived as lacking in competence, intelligence, and power.

MAUREEN MURDOCK

Sometimes when I'm feeling especially cynical, I notice exactly how much space my local newspaper has devoted to sports and cars and how little goes to spiritual growth and what I call *real* concerns.

AFFIRMATION

I seek beyond the popular for the growth and support I need.

DAY 43

In the world as it will be when women and men live in full partnership, there will, of course, still be families, schools, governments, and other social institutions. But like the already now emerging institutions of the equalitarian family and the social-action network, the social structures of the future will be based more on linking than ranking. Instead of requiring individuals that fit into pyramidal hierarchies, these institutions will be heterarchic, allowing for both diversity and flexibility in decision making and action. Consequently, the roles of both women and men will be far less rigid, allowing the entire human species a maximum of developmental flexibility.

RIANE EISLER

AFFIRMATION

I dream and work for the world that will be.

DAY 44

Insecure people think that all reality should be amenable to their paradigms. They have a high need to clone others, to mold them over into their own thinking. They don't realize that the very strength of the relationship is in having another point of view. Sameness is not oneness; uniformity is not unity. Unity, or oneness, is complementariness, not sameness. Sameness is uncreative . . . and boring. The essence of synergy is to value the differences.

STEPHEN R. COVEY

AFFIRMATION

I value differences.

DAY 45

Many people might think me unlucky because I am blind, and of course they are right in one way, but I prefer to think of myself as one of the lucky ones, which I am in relation to many blind people. Despite having been born into a highly conservative society and deprived of my sight by a combination of ignorance and superstition, I have nevertheless had the satisfaction and fulfillment of education and a profession—things which are denied to millions of women, blind and sighted, for a multitude of reasons but all too often because of economic and social backwardness. Indeed, I am lucky. The opportunity to make the best of things is held out, if we would only work for it. To quote Helen Keller, "I thank God for my handicaps, for through them I have found myself, my work, and my God."

LUCY CHING

AFFIRMATION

By using my opportunities to make the best of things, I choose to be "one of the lucky ones."

DAY 46

The pitcher cries for water to carry and a person for work that is real.

MARGE PIERCY

No one sits us down and says, "My dear, if you expect to be happy, find your Work." No one makes us understand that only work brings lasting respect in the world, self-esteem, purpose, and an organizing principle around which to order our lives. No one bothers to inform us that our Work may not pay us "diddly" yet may be the most joyful thing in our lives. No one tells us that finding our Work can be exasperating, disheartening, and that sometimes we can't even tell we've found it until we're halfway successful at it. Rarely is it written that our Work may be ephemeral, obscure, or its call so personal that ours are the only ears to hear it.

No one tells us that work and money and finances have their own rhythms and that we may have to make huge sacrifices for our Work or that, unexpectedly and after long labor, our Work may shower upon us the golden rain of money and the greater satisfaction of fulfilling our best potential.

AFFIRMATION

I open my heart to find my Work and my mind to figure out how to support it. And I help others do this.

DAY 47

Qualities students believe to be related to superior teaching:

1. *Stimulation of interest*
2. *Clarity*
3. *Knowledge of subject matter*
4. *Preparation*
5. *Enthusiasm*
6. *Friendliness*
7. *Helpfulness*
8. *Openness to other's opinions*

WILBERT J. MCKEACHIE

AFFIRMATION

I am a superior teacher.

DAY 48

Give attention (time and energy) to the positive and do not give attention (time and energy) to the negative.

CONNIE PODESTA

If you raised your voice when you wish you hadn't, ate that extra cookie, or neglected your exercise program for waste-of-time TV, now is the minute to withdraw—gently and easily—from the negative and to return full attention to your chosen path.

As Gerald May says about getting rid of bad habits in *Addiction and Grace*, it's "like getting rid of an alley cat. You don't have to kick it; just don't feed it."

This "path of meditation" can work well in a wide variety of situations. Try it to see if it suits you.

AFFIRMATION

I figure out how I want to behave and then I do it.

DAY 49

The girl was bright. She had an intelligence a notch and a half above the average, fairly strong on logic, rather literal in its demands, with, by the same token, a restless curiosity that made her trowel down to the essentials.

And she had what none of Alma's other pupils had: a deep belief that education was in her self-interest. . . . She retained what white America had generally shed for its myth of equality, an assumption that the mysteries in sign and serif, punctuation and print would get her on in the world.

JANET BURROWAY

AFFIRMATION

I like to teach and demonstrate the self-interest of education.

DAY 50

The first responsibility of a leader is to define reality. The last is to say thank you. In between the two, the leader must become a servant and a debtor. That sums up the progress of an artful leader.

MAX DE PREE

Defining reality is a tricky business. We can define reality as the present status quo and realize, of course, that there's no changing it. We can also define reality as a wished-for fantasy and, of course, sit back and wait for the dreams to materialize.

What we'll prefer to do—as leaders and inventors of our lives—is to find a middle path: an achievable reality that brings both satisfaction and motivation.

AFFIRMATION

Part of my reality is to always give others credit for help and ideas.

DAY 51

Daily encounters with turkeys cannot be avoided. Your best defense is to value yourself, your time, and your resources. When you learn to do that, saying no will be less painful and saying yes will be a pleasure. When turkeys get the best of you and you blow up, do not brood or punish yourself. Just take the experience as a reminder to tackle one turkey at a time.

MELODIE CHENEVERT

If you have problems with assertiveness, this oldie but goodie reference written for women in the health professions is a promising place to begin. From being called an "uppity nurse," to giving hints on dealing with arrogant men in power, to suggestions for how to protect the innocent, Melodie Chenevert has survived the fire—and with her sense of humor fully intact.

AFFIRMATION

I deal with turkeys without losing my cool.

DAY 52

The Four Great Myths of the White Male System: (1) the White Male System is the only thing that exists; (2) the White Male System is innately superior; (3) the White Male System knows and understands everything; and (4) the White Male System believes it is possible to be totally logical, rational, and objective.

ANNE WILSON SCHAEF

Anne Schaef goes on to add that living according to these myths can mean living in ignorance. For example, she says, "The only way to maintain the myth of knowing and understanding everything is to ignore a whole universe of other information. When one clings to the myth of innate superiority, one must constantly overlook the virtues and abilities of others."

AFFIRMATION

At deep levels, I am respectful of the virtues and abilities of others.

DAY 53

*Old managers, who used to tell the workers what to do and when to do
it, are finding themselves irrelevant because the workers are now in self-
managed work teams telling themselves what to do and when to do it.
Almost everything that managers were good at is now unnecessary. They
are back to zero. Small wonder most of the resistance to the Total Quality
programs comes from the middle managers.*

JOEL ARTHUR BARKER

As teachers, we always knew this. No one can take our place
in learning or in the classroom. No outmoded piece of paper or out-
dated set of rules can ever replace our real voices.

AFFIRMATION

*I strive for excellence and to discover measures to tell me when I
reach it.*

DAY 54

*Tom Melohn understands that the central issue facing our organizations
today—an issue that must be addressed—is how to release the brain power,
the know-how of the work force. [Education] Companies are going to fall
or rise on whether or not they recognize that it's going to take brains, ideas,
knowledge that will create innovation, re-invention and result in successful performance.*

WARREN BENNIE
(QUOTED IN MELOHN)

It's also pointed out here that whips and chains won't un-
block talent and that you/we will have to "create an environment of
respect, caring, integrity, high standards and, above all, trust."

AFFIRMATION

*I search widely for information that will help me help invent the
future. (Even if that means rediscovering the past!)*

DAY 55

The place to learn about moral courage is in our personal lives—doing what we believe is right and not being subservient to the opinion of others. If we can instill a sense of moral courage in our youth, they will have the confidence to resist those peer pressures that promote drugs, violence, and other destructive behavior.

KESHAVAN NAIR

Here it is again—that ever-perennial idea that to instill moral courage in others, we'll have to demonstrate it ourselves. How utterly tiresome and unfair—we're going to have to practice what we preach!

The splendid news, though, is that we don't have to travel any further than ourselves to begin.

AFFIRMATION

Today I recommit to moral courage in my personal life.

DAY 56

Unless a person takes charge of them, both work and free time are likely to be disappointing. Most jobs and many leisure activities—especially those involving the passive consumption of mass media—are not designed to make us happy and strong. Their purpose is to make money for someone else. If we allow them to, they can suck out the marrow of our lives, leaving only feeble husks. But like everything else, work and leisure can be appropriated for our needs. People who learn to enjoy their work, who do not waste their free time, end up feeling that their lives as a whole have become much more worthwhile. "The future," wrote C. K. Brightbill, "will belong not only to the educated person, but to the person who is educated to use their leisure wisely." (Masculine nouns made generic.)

MIHALY CSIKSZENTMIHALYI

AFFIRMATION

I am an educated person who uses work and leisure time wisely.

DAY 57

No one has the "right" to degrade, shame, or humiliate another person in public or in private. And no one has the "responsibility" to sit still and take such abuse. It is time to develop a BM Award (Bad Manners, of course) to be given at moments when words are inadequate to express the proper feeling. . . . A temper tantrum is a temper tantrum, whether the person involved is a toddler or an eminent brain surgeon. . . . The rough, the rude, the noisy, the nosey, the bitch, the bully, the gossip, and the grouch—give them all BM stickers.

MELODIE CHENEVERT

Dealing with people who intrude in our space is a major life task. Review your techniques and successes. Begin changing what doesn't please you.

AFFIRMATION

I stick up for myself.

DAY 58

In my definition, any woman who regards her life as her own and who doesn't want someone else to make her decisions for her (on either a personal or a political level) is a feminist.

REGINA BARRECA

Or as Rebecca West said in 1913, "I myself have never been able to find precisely what feminism is. I only know that people call me a feminist whenever I express sentiments that differentiate me from a doormat" (quoted in *A Feminist Dictionary* by Kramarae and Treichler).

Because teaching comes recently from a "women's work" category, some old attitudes may be lying around and getting in the way. Because we're conscious and conscientious, it may be our task (and pleasure!) to help sweep them out of the way.

AFFIRMATION

Calling myself a feminist becomes easier and easier.

DAY 59

People are nonliving when angry, depressed, feeling sorry for themselves, or filled with fear.

MARLO MORGAN

If we really thought of ourselves as nonliving—which we probably are—when we are angry, depressed, feeling sorry for ourselves, and fearful, then we would surely work a lot harder to get ourselves out of these negative states.

AFFIRMATION

I am always living.

DAY 60

The manner in which we respond to negative criticism is a clue to the level of our self-esteem. If we harbor a feeling of inadequacy, negative criticism can wipe us out. Most of us carry with us too many internalized low-esteem messages from the past, negative things our parents or siblings or teachers or schoolday peers said to us.

ELISABETH RUEDY AND SUE NIRENBERG

Elisabeth Ruedy is right when she tell us that our inner voices need new songs and new sentences to maneuver us through tough spots and to help keep us afloat through the day. She suggests that it is most productive to work daily with one affirmation that really speaks to us until it becomes comfortable and natural. *I am brilliant* is one she finds helps many of her clients with severe math anxiety. *I am comfortable dealing with power* is one I use. Affirmations can be used by teachers and students.

AFFIRMATION

I receive appropriate criticism without loss of self-esteem.

DAY 61

The singing of my self fills every empty space within the universe and I re-member who I am.

MARILYN GALTIN

This week I consider again the discipline and growth of meditation—perhaps reading a book I already have, checking out one from the library, or deepening my ongoing practice.

AFFIRMATION

I listen and discover how I am called to serve.
I listen and remember who I am.

DAY 62

What is our responsibility toward evolution? To continue this beautiful life process. If you take this on, life becomes very precious. Even the things you dislike most about your life become precious. Go outside and look at a rose and smell it, or look at a baby to know what I mean.

We are curators of all life on this planet. We hold it in our hands. It is a beautiful planet, maybe the only life in the whole universe, and I refuse to believe we are silly enough to destroy it.

HELEN CALDICOTT
(QUOTED IN VETTER)

Aubury Wallace, in *Green Means: Living Gently on the Planet*, says that by the time an average American reaches age 75, she or he has used five times as much energy as the world average—and generated 52 tons of garbage.

AFFIRMATION

I am responsible for seven generations times seven generations to come. My teaching can reach this far and further.

DAY 63

This boy is Ignorance. This girl is Want. Beware of them both, and all of their degree, but most of all beware this boy, for on his brow I see that written which is Doom, unless the writing be erased.

CHARLES DICKENS

AFFIRMATION

I enjoy erasing Doom from the foreheads of children and young adults.

DAY 64

"Willie, you copied this essay out of a book, this book." I hold up a popular anthology from the library.

"Gee, Miss Giardino, didn't I do what you wanted? Oh. Well, can I make it up?"

"I do not allow make-up on plagiarized papers."

"Plag . . . I don't understand those big words. What does that mean?"

"It means you got an F on that."

Sometimes he turns in nothing at all. "I didn't know how to do it, Miss G."

"Stay after school and I'll help you."

"And miss football practice!" The whole class laughs. He expects me to fall into the accommodation that all the other teachers have made: Willie must have a C in order that he play football. Give him a C and he will smile cheerfully and make no trouble.

Insist that he earn the C, and there will be trouble.

DOROTHY BRYANT

AFFIRMATION

I have a personal answer for this dilemma.

DAY 65

I do not believe that disciplined reflection takes time away from work; it sustains the spirit and increases the intensity and quality of work.

KESHAVAN NAIR

Just as regular exercise, a decent diet, enough sleep, and a positive attitude literally do increase our available energy, so does disciplined reflection (meditation) increase our focus and the "intensity and quality of [our] work."

AFFIRMATION

I understand the value of and I practice disciplined reflection.

DAY 66

There are pragmatic reasons for all of us to focus on our responsibilities rather than our rights.

A society driven by responsibilities is oriented toward service, acknowledging other points of view, compromise, and progress—whereas a society driven by rights is oriented toward acquisition, confrontation, and advocacy. If we . . . treat others as ourselves, the fabric of society does not have to be threatened in the struggle to achieve rights.

KESHAVAN NAIR

AFFIRMATION

I make the effort to understand how societies operate and what the possible consequences from society's rules and mores are.

DAY 67

Joe [Campbell] was convinced that we were about to remythologize our-selves. "A new mythos is coming," he used to say. "A global one, Mickey. I don't know how it will come or what it will be . . ."

MICKEY HART

This is what teachers always face—that at some level our students always know more than we do for we can only speculate about the future. They are living it. This can be a tragedy of parents, that the generation they best prepare us to live in is their own. But we, of course, already reside in a more complex world, growing more so every minute.

AFFIRMATION

I use the best of the past to live better in the present and to prepare for the future.

DAY 68

Such a man might like the abstract idea of marriage, but he doesn't want the aggravation of having a real live wife. He wants the convenience of a home and hearth without wanting the emotional responsibility of its up-keep. It's like wanting to eat a great meal without cooking or cleaning up, or wanting to be a great musician without practicing. Sure, as a fantasy it's terrific. As a plan for life, it's a disaster.

REGINA BARRECA

A lot of us want perfect education for all. But we don't want the aggravation and responsibility for getting it.

AFFIRMATION

I pay all necessary costs for education, including intellectual and emotional, social and financial.

DAY 69

Self-esteem should be SELF-esteem. What you think of yourself is much more important than what others think of you. Ugly duckling or swan? You are the only person who can answer. Somewhere along the road to assertiveness lies self-acceptance.

> *This is it!*
> *This is me!*
> *The only me there'll ever be!*
> *How long has it been since you spent some time with yourself?*
> MELODIE CHENEVERT

AFFIRMATION

I care for myself and I take care of myself. I am a treasure.

DAY 70

Little tiny lies. Men who tell their wives they earn a hundred and fifty a week when they make two hundred; wives who tell their men the shoes cost twenty-five in a sale when they were forty-two fifty. Sons who tell their ma's they were at Sunday school; daughters who've been to the pictures with a girl friend. . . . The mothers will lie to whitewash the whole family.

I expect it. I sit waiting for a moment to tell them what fools they're making of themselves. Lying is never courage or self-sacrifice, it's nothing but cowardice and self-deception all the way. You're hiding something from your wife rather than from me; have the guts to come out with it and take a weight off her mind. As for me, I'm conducting a murder investigation. I've now no further time for liars. Especially the worst kind, and that's you. The kind that lie to dramatize themselves.

> NICOLAS FREELING

AFFIRMATION

I give myself the gift of honesty.

DAY 71

Remarkable and eccentric and imperfect as they are, our days and our nights are the only things we fully own, the only things over which we have any measure of control, and we all too often betray and abandon these days to longing, misery, anger, or disappointment. . . . Not until my early thirties did I realize that I was fully responsible for my own choices and decisions and happiness; healthy and able, I had no business trafficking in misery.

REGINA BARRECA

"A life of integrity is the most fundamental source of personal worth," says Stephen Covey. He says we can't psych ourselves into peace of mind—which comes "when your life is in harmony with true principles and values and in no other way."

AFFIRMATION

I leave any misery far behind and continue getting my life in order. And finding my heart/soul/spirit.

DAY 72

Being *requires accepting oneself, staying within oneself and not **doing** to prove oneself. It is a discipline that is accorded no applause from the outside world; it questions production for production's sake. Politically and economically it has little value, but its simple message has wisdom: If I can accept myself as I am, and if I am in harmony with my surroundings, I have no need to produce, promote, or pollute to be happy. And being is not passive; it takes focused awareness.*

MAUREEN MURDOCK

AFFIRMATION

I am in harmony with myself and my surroundings.

DAY 73

One thing became clear to me once we started down the road to shared power: The more skilled our co-workers were, the more effective they would be. As noted earlier, responsibility without competence gets you nowhere but in trouble. So I began to look for ways to help the group at NATD [his company] increase their technical competence.

TOM MELOHN

As Tom Melohn says, "We forged a new partnership with our co-workers simply by hiring good people who care and treating them just the way we want to be treated."

To gather some allies for change, you might want to take a look at Tom Melohn's book—also Max De Pree's *Leadership Is an Art* and perhaps Bolman and Deal's *Leading With Soul.*

AFFIRMATION

I forge new partnerships with my co-workers.

DAY 74

The easiest person to deceive is one's own self.

BULWER-LYTTON
(QUOTED IN FINGARETTE)

Even yet a favorite poem I wrote a long time ago evokes a smile of recognition:

Never lie
to yourself.

But always
expect yourself
to try.

Think for a few moments about how you keep yourself on the straight and narrow.

AFFIRMATION

While I may not always tell everyone everything, I never deceive myself.

DAY 75

Good character consists of knowing the good, desiring the good, and doing the good—habits of the mind, habits of the heart, and habits of action. All three are necessary for leading a moral life: all three make up moral maturity.

THOMAS LICKONA

AFFIRMATION

I strive for moral maturity.

DAY 76

Livelihood is the central core around which most people build their lives. There are exceptions, of course. But the majority of human beings, notably in industrial communities, dedicate their best hours and their best years to getting an income and exchanging it for the necessaries and decencies of physical and social existence.

HELEN AND SCOTT NEARING

Buddhism in right livelihood says we should make our living in ways that do not harm others. (In other words, in this day and age cigarette makers and drug dealers are in moral danger.) Marsha Sinetar speaks to this subject of money in *A Way Without Words: A Guide for Spiritually Emerging Adults.* She says she's found people making $5,000 a year who've been able to design lives that please them, and she's met people making over $250,000 a year who are unable to give up anything for a life they say they would prefer.

AFFIRMATION

I am happy with how I earn my living.

As I looked into Carmen's eyes that evening, I saw a timelessness, a warm, primitive presence capable of filling a vast emptiness, like smoke from a comforting campfire that almost lingers long enough to mend a broken heart.

I poured a couple get-acquainted shots from a bottle of Wild Turkey. . . . Over the years I'd developed a hard-hewn code of ethics; not only did I live by it, but I felt that without it, life itself would have very little meaning for me. On the other hand, I wasn't running for the school board.

KINKY FRIEDMAN

The *I Ching* (Reifler) tells us that if our own principles are vague we will be more likely to tolerate basically uncongenial and unsuitable situations.

Nowhere does ethics get more complicated than when we're dealing with real, live people. And these ethical questions are frequently aggravated by dropping our unprotected heads without warning. We'll be wise to develop a "hard-hewn code of ethics"—and even wiser to understand when to hold tight to that code of ethics, and when we aren't "running for the school board"!

AFFIRMATION

More and more, I know when to raise (as in poker), when to play, and when to fold.

DAY 78

For those who say I can't impose my morality on others, I say just watch me.
JOSEPH SCHEIDLER, DIRECTOR OF THE PRO-LIFE LEAGUE
(QUOTED IN REICH)

It has taken me a long time to understand that vehemence, belief, and sincerity are no guarantees of truth. Just because they believe it does not make it so. Just because I believe it does not make it so. Still, there's a lot to be said for allowing differing beliefs—and not resorting to violence, which never really changes, in a positive way, anybody's mind or heart.

AFFIRMATION

I examine moral issues for their underlying truths.
And their consequences, which are also truths.

DAY 79

The quest for excellence automatically opens up the quest for innovation. Innovation takes us into territories we have never been to before; and therefore, to be responsible to the future and to the things we value, we must develop a sense of anticipation of the implications of our innovations. This will allow us to pick from the many potential solutions to our problems and find the few that best support those values we wish to carry into the future.
JOEL ARTHUR BARKER

Three keys for the twenty-first century, says Joel Barker in this thought-provoking work, are anticipation, innovation, and excellence.

AFFIRMATION

My work is not separate from me, nor am I separate from my responsibility for what grows from my work.

DAY 80

The single step of doing one act of personal service every day will keep you in direct contact with the overarching work of leadership: service.

KESHAVAN NAIR

Keshavan Nair relates how, early on, Gandhi once took a leper into his home to care for him. But Gandhi soon realized he couldn't care for the leper and do the other things he also felt were necessary. Gandhi ended up putting the leper in a government hospital and rearranging his legal work so that he could spend two hours a day at a local free hospital presenting patient complaints to the doctor and dispensing medicines. "This work," Gandhi wrote, "brought me some peace."

AFFIRMATION

I do one act of personal service every day.

DAY 81

The most challenging dragon of all, however, is the societal reptile that smiles and says, "Yes dear, you can do anything you want to do," while continuing to sabotage her progress with few opportunities, low salaries, inadequate child care, and slow promotions. What this dragon really means is, "Yes dear, you can do anything you want to do as long as you do what we want you to do."

MAUREEN MURDOCK

AFFIRMATION

I know how to kill dragons.

DAY 82

The Daily Private Victory—a minimum of one hour a day in renewal of the physical, spiritual, and mental dimensions—is the key to the development of the Seven Habits and it's completely within your Circle of influence. It is the . . . focus time necessary to integrate these habits into your life, to become principle-centered.

STEPHEN R. COVEY

Over and over, we return to the concern of actually getting ourselves to do what we've decided to do—to consistently put our dreams into action. One way is to experiment until we find what works for us. Perhaps we must do our chosen new behavior first thing in the morning. Perhaps we must offer ourselves a bribe of saying we won't take a treat until we've disposed of an unwanted project. Perhaps we need to treat ourselves as intrepid experimenters and say we'll try this project for a month and then give it up or find a better way if it doesn't work as we'd hoped.

AFFIRMATION

I always have enough time and energy to do what I want to do. Or be specific; fill in your blank—walk every day. Meditate. Exercise. Eat right. Listen. Treat others with respect and love.

DAY 83

After prolonged research on myself, I brought out the fundamental duplicity
of the human being. Then I realized, as a result of delving in my memory,
that modesty helped me to shine, humility to conquer, and virtue to oppress.

A. CAMUS

I examine the back roads of myself to discover my duplicity.
For example, am I so "virtuous" others become afraid to share themselves with me?

AFFIRMATION

More and more, I come to terms with my duplicity.

DAY 84

Purity of heart is to will one thing and to will it absolutely—it is the self as
the unity of the entire individual acknowledged as self; it is thus the found-
ing of the eternal, of that which endures through change and even within
change; it is the condition of the truly ethical life, and ultimately of the
truly saving religious life.

HERBERT FINGARETTE

Some days I feel like taking an opinion poll of my disparate
selves. This one wants fame. That one wants love. This one desires
only money. That one wants to give everything away. This one wishes
devoutly to crawl into a narrow, quiet room with library books
stacked to the ceiling and never emerge.

On better days the clear voice from meditation murmurs that my
task is to write from the heart.

AFFIRMATION

More and more, I live and work from the heart.

DAY 85

I have identified five basic commitments that lead to a higher standard of leadership:

Develop a basis for the single standard: Commit to absolute values.
Acknowledge the ideal: Commit to the journey.
Develop the guide that will keep you on the journey: Commit to training your conscience.
Reduce forces that lead you astray: Commit to reducing attachments.
Be willing to stand scrutiny: Commit to minimizing secrecy.

KESHAVAN NAIR

Interestingly, Nair says that a trained conscience is developed through personal reflection. He reminds us, though, that without a commitment to the truth, personal reflection will result only in rationalization.

AFFIRMATION

I aim for a higher standard of leadership through commitment to truth.

DAY 86

*Ed's [Ricketts] interest in music was passionate and profound. He loved the secular passion of Monteverde, and the sharpness of Scarlatti. His was a very broad appreciation and a curiosity that dug for music as he dug for his delicious worms in a mud flat. He listened to music with his mouth open as though he wanted to receive the tones even in his throat. His forefinger moved secretly at his side in rhythm. . . . He once told me that he thought the **Art of the Fugue** of Bach might be the greatest of all music up to our time. Always "up to our time." He never considered anything finished or completed but always continuing, one thing growing on and out of another.*

JOHN STEINBECK

To be able to lose ourselves in music, in tennis, in painting, in a play, in a book, in an absorbing movie—how lucky we are. Our lives are enriched and our duties are lightened.

AFFIRMATION

I have interests that enrich and absorb me utterly.

DAY 87

*People tend to look at things without really seeing them. They block out the unfamiliar and allow access only to what they feel comfortable with. **Focus your awareness to discover things you have overlooked and things that others don't see.***

NITA LELAND

I was driving down a back road once with a museum curator who pointed to a distant porch and said, "Look at the finial on that chair, probably made around the 1860s." Later that week, I drove with an enthusiast who spied a car on blocks through an open barn door and cried, "That's a Model T and in great condition." Left to my own devices, I'd have seen neither chair nor car. But I did begin noticing how I always pointed out wildflowers along the highway and how a particular tree stood out from the rest.

AFFIRMATION

I see with fresh eyes.
I practice seeing.

DAY 88

Every teacher sees this happen. I know I did. When I was explaining a concept to my students, many were unable to understand it even though the information was directly in front of them. But, as they began to understand the principles, they would say, one by one, "Oh, now I get it." What they were getting was the paradigm; what they were gaining was a significant change in vision.

JOEL ARTHUR BARKER

Here is the heart of teaching—enlarging minds, helping others change vision and perspective.

AFFIRMATION

My focus is on new paradigms and changes in vision.

DAY 89

Key Characteristics of Paradigms: 1) Paradigms are common, 2) Paradigms are functional, 3) The paradigm effect reverses the common sense relationship between seeing and believing, 4) There is almost always more than one right answer, 5) Paradigms too strongly held can lead to paradigm paralysis, a terminal disease of certainty, 6) Paradigm pliancy is the best strategy in turbulent times, 7) Human beings can choose to change their paradigms.

JOEL ARTHUR BARKER

Paradigms are models, patterns, rules, regulations, how the world is supposed to be. A powerful business example of a paradigm shift is IBM and Apple computers. IBM owned the computer world— their big main-frame computers (only to be touched by experts) got bigger and more powerful. Enter a paradigm shift and small personal Apple computers that ordinary people can take out of boxes and use. Before the clash was over, IBM had climbed off its exclusive high horse and joined Apple in the personal computer market. And the world had changed.

AFFIRMATION

I learn about paradigms and how I can better use them.

DAY 90

Truth is truth. If you hurt someone, you hurt self. If you help someone, you help self. . . . Real people think about forever. It's all one, our ancestors, our unborn grandchildren, all of life everywhere.

MARLO MORGAN

AFFIRMATION

At times I am the leaf; at times I am the tree.

The first process I want to explore here is paradox. . . . Paradox is not linear, and it cannot be measured by numbers. . . . All of the major world religions emphasize the importance of surrender. In its own way, surrender is paradox. To seek power is to lose it. To surrender power is to gain it. It may not be the same sort of power we were looking for to begin with; it may be worth even more.

Paradox often emerges in childrearing. If we try to control and hold on to our children, we lose them. If we let them go, they return to us more fully.

It is very hard for White Male System persons to allow paradox to take its place in their lives. Doing so implies a certain lessening of control, and it is difficult for a superior being to go along with this.

ANNE WILSON SCHAEF

Anne Schaef reminds us that when someone tells us we have to do (1) this or (2) that, we can notice and point out that we could also do this (3) or that (4) and we can encourage others to come up with further creative possible solutions.

AFFIRMATION

I am mindful of who is controlling, who has power, and what they do with it.

When an educational program or technique doesn't yield the expected results it typically meets one of three fates: it's abandoned, it's analyzed again and again by successions of more- or less-qualified people who typically have little ability to enact real solutions, or it's patched with the easiest, quickest, and least expensive repair to be found. The reason is that unlike virtually all other professions, U.S. education lacks a technical culture, a common body of proven knowledge and technique that lets all members of a profession adapt and perform to the same standards of excellence, and to redefine those standards as technology progresses.

KENNETH G. WILSON

Kenneth Wilson makes excellent points as he contrasts how the United States supports its farmers in looking for new ways to boost harvest. Farmers are free to experiment and use their own techniques; farmers are constantly talking with other farmers, trading insights and experiences; they talk with knowledgeable salespeople to learn new products and ways; they visit showrooms and meet their county extension agent. In short, the farmer has "access to a network of experts . . . that exists expressly to find better ways for him to farm." And when the farmer gets in trouble, we expect the farmer to be involved in diagnosing and fixing the problem.

AFFIRMATION

Education is my profession and my job.
I get involved and I stay involved.

DAY 93

Including and adhering to moral criteria in developing strategy . . . requires qualities of the spirit that are in all of us irrespective of race, gender, creed, or origin.

KESHAVAN NAIR

Nair also writes that at a personal level, Gandhi's commitment was to a moral life and that Gandhi defined his personal achievement by his adherence to the moral criteria of truth and nonviolence, paying little attention to economic considerations. "We must ask ourselves what we are willing to do to be successful."

AFFIRMATION

I take individual responsibility for my moral standards and growth.

DAY 94

Too much is never enough.

MARK TWAIN'S COMMENT ON BOURBON

No wise person, of course, will pay the price of addiction. When we are trapped, our first task in life is obviously to get rid of addiction—to stay in the place of pain, and learning, until we are free of the addiction. (And, it's worth noting, we define for ourselves which are addictions and which are harmless habits better left alone.)

Perhaps the more striking tragedy, though, is being burned by another's addictions. AA's saying helps me: God [Goddess, the Universe], grant me the serenity to accept the things I cannot change, the courage to change the things I can, and the wisdom to know the difference. (And there are also many support groups where we can get information and help.) Part of our wisdom also may come from reading books like *Classrooms Under the Influence: Addicted Families/Addicted Students* by Powell, Zehm, and Kottler, a compilation that brings insight and help.

AFFIRMATION

I am a wise person.

15 Traits of a healthy family: (1) communicates and listens, (2) affirms and supports one another, (3) teaches respect for others, (4) develops a sense of trust, (5) has a sense of play and humor, (6) exhibits a sense of shared responsibility, (7) teaches a sense of right and wrong, (8) has a strong sense of family in which rituals and traditions abound, (9) has a balance of interaction among members, (10) has a shared religious core, (11) respects the privacy of one another, (12) values service to others, (13) fosters table time and conversation, (14) shares leisure time, (15) admits to and seeks help with problems.

DOLORES CURRAN

AFFIRMATION

I know the traits of a healthy family, and I practice adding these traits into my life.

DAY 96

Vitamin C also promotes restful sleep. A study measuring possible brain and central-nervous-system stimulants and sedatives demonstrated that vitamin C has potent sedative, antianxiety properties.

JOAN MATHEWS LARSON

We can use nutrition to help ourselves and others. According to *Diet for a New America*, quoted in *50 Simple Things You Can Do to Save the Earth* by the Earthworks Group, if Americans reduced their meat intake by just 10%, the savings in grains and soybeans could adequately feed 60 million people—the number of people who starve to death, worldwide, each year. We can use nutrition to help ourselves and others.

AFFIRMATION

I study enough nutrition from enough different reputable sources to maintain my healthy body, mind, and spirit—and the environment.

DAY 97

I've been in the storm so long, children
been in the storm so long
I've been in the storm so long, children
gimme a little time to pray.

AFRICAN AMERICAN SPIRITUAL
(QUOTED IN MORRISON-REED AND JAMES)

Sometimes it's hard to hear our own voice with all the competing ones. And sometimes our own self-righteousness can be a barrier. "Nothing so needs reforming as other people's habits," Mark Twain reminds us in *Pudd'nhead Wilson.* And what's all that business about motes and beams? That I can't see the mote in your eye because of the beam in mine? Or as Robert Pirsig puts it in *Lila: An Inquiry Into Morals,* "Vice is a conflict between biological quality and social quality. Things like sex and booze and drugs and tobacco have a high biological quality, that is, they feel good, but are harmful for social reasons. They take all your money. They break up your family. They threaten the stability of the community."

AFFIRMATION

All my efforts in reforming habits begin with my own.

DAY 98

Teachers have the power to affect the values and character of the young in at least three ways:

1. *Teachers can serve as effective caregivers . . .*
2. *Teachers can serve as models . . .*
3. *Teachers can serve as ethical mentors . . .*

THOMAS LICKONA

AFFIRMATION

I am an effective and ethical caregiver model.

DAY 99

I'm into quick foods. If I can't burn it in five minutes or less, I won't bother. . . . The last time I served fresh-squeezed orange juice was when someone accidentally stepped on a bag of Valencias. To me, "homemade" means you've had to thaw it.

MARTHA BOLTON

Time to many is becoming more precious than gold. How do you find time to do what you want to do when you're already doing more than you can do?

You do the ordinary things—make priority lists, read some books on time management, get rid of stuff, and learn to say and mean *No*. At some point you realize that you alone own your days and your nights. If you don't spend your minutes and hours as you want, someone else will spend them for you; you'll end up living your only life as you don't want to live it.

AFFIRMATION

I own my time and I spend it as I wish.

DAY 100

I thought of people at home in the United States: the number of young people who seemed to have no sense of direction or purpose, the homeless people who think they have nothing to offer society, the addicted individuals who want to function in some reality other than the one we are in. I wished I could bring them here [to outback Australia], to witness how little it takes, sometimes, to be a benefit to your community, and how wonderful it is to know and experience a sense of self-worth.

MARLO MORGAN

"Garbage is just a test we must pass to move toward new discovery. Sooner or later, all pain and vulnerability, all garbage, must be regarded as an opportunity for new learning," says Carl Hammerschlag in *The Theft of the Spirit*.

AFFIRMATION

I have positive self-worth and I am a benefit to my community.

DAY 101

Spirituality has too long been an almost exclusively male realm, resting in abstract principle and institutionalized order. In contrast, women tend towards a relational sacrality that is based on the natural world of earth and flesh. The woman's perspective is healing and life-giving, one that we can ill afford to ignore.

MARILYN SEWELL

There is no excuse, is there, for not broadening our knowledge, for not seeing the messes a male-ordered society has produced, and for not looking for better ways. For example, *The Feminine Face of God* takes an in-depth look at 200 contemporary women (mostly unknown) who are living spiritual-based lives. Authors Sherry Anderson and Patricia Hopkins look for communality and for how these women acquired and currently live their spirituality.

AFFIRMATION

More and more, my spirituality becomes a part of my life.

DAY 102

I am personally thankful that we live together in a large moral house even if we do not drink at the same fountain of faith. The world we experience together is one world, God's [Goddess's] world, and our world, and the problems we share are common human problems. So we can talk together, try to understand each other, and help each other.

LEWIS B. SMEDES

We were "never called to build kingdoms," that is, to do everything ourselves, to quote Natalie Kusz's autobiographical novel, *Road Song.* She was mauled by a bear in Alaska, which took many years and operations to heal, and so learned the immense patience that was required to put her life back together.

AFFIRMATION

I work toward one world.

DAY 103

The young delinquents in question are those who frankly engage in behavior which society forbids as immoral or illegal, and who do so not out of some deep commitment of their own, but irresponsibly. . . . [August] Aichorn came to see them as persons who had not developed strong super-egos; they had not internalized parental and cultural moral demands. Thus appeals to conscience, to a concern for human values, were of course to no avail.

HERBERT FINGARETTE

"There are no chains more vicious than the chains of biological necessity into which every child is born," says Robert Pirsig in *Lila: An Inquiry Into Morals.* "Society exists primarily to free people from these biological chains. It has done that job so stunningly well intellectuals forget the fact and turn upon society with a shameful ingratitude for what society has done."

What is society, what is biology, and which human values do we support?

AFFIRMATION

I help free people from the chains of biological necessity. I do not look for easy answers to hard questions, but I do look for answers.

DAY 104

Compassion and humility may be among the most treasured of human virtues, but they are not useful in conflict. . . . Virtue is to be valued in the proper context; only a sword will do in battle.

DENG MING-DAO

Unless you are very unusual, you never started out to do battle—yours was to be a calm, ordered existence where everyone knew the kind and gentle rules and obeyed them.

That placid world is no more. When children and young adults grow up in personal chaos, it's easy for them to mistake kindness and care for weakness and vulnerability. And it's sometimes hard for us to remember that not every encounter is a therapeutic one—with us being the accommodator!

AFFIRMATION

In battle, I remember to bring along my sword.

DAY 105

The 12 Principles of Character: (1) honesty, (2) understanding, (3) compassion and empathy, (4) appreciation, (5) patience, (6) discipline, (7) fortitude, (8) perseverance, (9) humor, (10) humility, (11) generosity, (12) respect.

KATHRYN B. JOHNSON

How long since you asked yourself, "What is character? What are my strong points of character? What am I doing to improve my weak ones? How am I teaching character?"

AFFIRMATION

Today, and for as long as I need, I ponder character.

DAY 106

Summing up the Case for Values Education:

1. *There is a clear and urgent need.*
2. *Transmitting values is and always has been the work of civilization.*
3. *The school's role as moral educator becomes even more vital at a time when millions of children get little moral teaching from their parents and where value-centered influences such as church or temple are also absent from their lives.*
4. *There is common ethical ground even in our value-conflicted society.*
5. *Democracies have a special need for moral education, because democracy is government by the people themselves.*
6. *There is no such thing as value-free education.*
7. *The great questions facing both the individual person and the human race are moral questions.*
8. *There is broad-based, growing support for values education in the schools.*
9. *An unabashed commitment to moral education is essential if we are to attract and keep good teachers.*

THOMAS LICKONA

AFFIRMATION

I know how I feel about Values Education, and I practice what I preach.

DAY 107

To educate a person in mind and not in morals is to educate a menace to society.

THEODORE ROOSEVELT
(QUOTED IN LICKONA)

When chaos rules, civilization dies. When repression and bigotry rule, people die.

AFFIRMATION

I support education of mind and morals.

DAY 108

Take them away from the graves of their ancestors, force them to abandon the spirits in every tree—to the Indians it's like taking away their soul. Separate an Indian from his tribe, his family, and you break his will. All that has been done on purpose. What you see lying around are not braves any more, but hoboes. Some politician in Washington worked it all out, then locked his desk and went home to kiss his wife, hug his children, and stroke his dog.

JAN DE HARTOG

A wise friend used to tell me that she couldn't challenge a student's beliefs. "Because," she said, "I don't have anything to replace them with." I would reply with my observation that I had required the structure of religion until I was strong enough to search for my personal brand of spirituality.

AFFIRMATION

I cherish the beliefs of others as I do my own.

DAY 109

I know we each have two lives: the one we learn by and the one we live after that.

MARLO MORGAN

We come to consciousness at different times and speeds. Crying and wailing and saying we've wasted our lives can be a big temptation. We can also use that first waste as an excuse to continue wasting our lives. Or we can do our version of the tobacco lobbyist, Victor Crawford, who is now declaring, "I was on the wrong side. Believe me now . . . as I'm dying of lung cancer."

Disillusion and finally growing up (at least to our present level of awareness) can be tough. Our real question is: How do we live after we learn? To come to terms, some of us even write books; I wrote *The End of Motherhood* out of an absolute determination to take my pain and make something useful of it.

AFFIRMATION

I live and learn, learn and act.

*Not all American white people are alike, but it is noteworthy that on all
this journey [through Europe in 1913] during all these months the only
snobs we met were some of our fellow-Americans. Mrs. Avery is white and
Mrs. Pickens light of skin, so that my face served as the only cue to these
snobs. . . . Whenever any one glared as we entered a dining-room, or tried
to spread himself out over three or four seats when we entered a vehicle, we
knew where he was from. . . . Some of it was ludicrous. We had great fun.*

WILLIAM PICKENS

William Pickens, born in 1881, was the sixth of ten children
and the first son born to Jacob and Fannie Pickens, former slaves who
gained their freedom after the fall of the Confederacy in 1865. He was
a Phi Beta Kappa graduate of Yale and became a nationally recognized African American leader, one of the half-dozen best-known
Black men of his time.

AFFIRMATION

I cultivate grace and fairness in dealing with others.

DAY 111

There is only one view-point which is justifiable and natural; to take up one's position in life itself, to look at it from the inside, and to see if it feels itself decadent, that is to say, diminished, weakened, insipid.

JOSÉ ORTEGA Y GASSET

Ortega y Gasset shows another way to evaluate ourselves, what's going on around us, and our lives. At any point, we can simply stop the action and ask ourselves how we feel. My life lately—is it healthy? Does it have soul? Am I happy? Or, instead, do I feel "diminished, weakened, insipid"?

AFFIRMATION

First, I name for myself how I feel. Then I plan what I will do about it.

DAY 112

The potential entrepreneur [or educator] becomes aware of the uselessness of much of her work or life, seeing that this uselessness conflicts with her moral imperative to live a more meaningful life. Women who have evolved to a high level of motivation and health desperately seek self-fulfillment. If at this moment they have insight into the solution for what it is that dissatisfies them and the energy to focus intensively on a single issue for five years, they will become entrepreneurs. [Or educators. Or whatever they choose to be.] This is what is meant by heart.

A. DAVID SILVER

AFFIRMATION

I live a self-fulfilled and meaningful life. I teach others to do the same.

DAY 113

The things you see in that individual that you admire are qualities within yourself that you wish to make more dominant. The actions, appearances, and behavior that you do not like are things about yourself that need working on.

MARLO MORGAN

The aboriginals believe the only way persons ever truly change anything about themselves is by their own decisions and that we all have the ability to change anything we want to about our personality. Morgan goes on to say, "There is no limit to what you can release and what you can acquire. They also believe the only true influence you have on anyone else is by your own life, how you act, what you do. Believing this way makes the tribal members committed every day to being better persons."

AFFIRMATION

I am committed every day to being a better person.

DAY 114

Think about education: Put on your VRG (virtual reality gear) in chemistry and with your teacher by your "virtual" side, you can investigate the concept of atoms. . . . Think about geography. Now you can go to see the Amazon, the barrens of Asia, the mountains of the moon. Think about mathematics; finally you will be able to see rendered in three dimensions what all those quadratic equations look like.

JOEL ARTHUR BARKER

And just think—probably in our very lifetimes we'll be able to go to our library and take out free "virtual" copies!

AFFIRMATION

I love to use modern technology—even if I'm not yet perfect.

By viewing a drop of whole blood, it is possible to see many aspects of patients' chemistry graphically in movement. We connected the microscope to a video camera and monitor screen. Sitting next to the physician, patients could see their white cells, red cells, bacteria, or fat in the background. I would take samples, show the patients their blood, and then ask smokers, for instance, to step outside and have a cigarette. After only a few moments, we would draw another sample, and they could see what effects that one cigarette had. The system is used for patient education and is very powerful in motivating them toward becoming responsible for their own welfare.

MARLO MORGAN

Marlo Morgan adds in this fiction/nonfiction work that doctors as educators can use this microscope, video, and monitor screen method to show people the level of fat in their blood or a sluggish immune response, and then can talk about what people can do to help themselves. (Of course, in the United States, our insurance companies so far won't cover costs for preventive measures.)

AFFIRMATION

I educate myself globally so I can support my beliefs locally.

DAY 116

I pondered the situation as objectively as I could and came to the conclusion that lack of vision was, undeniably, a great limitation but if other blind people could manage I must not allow myself to say "I can't." What I had to say was "How can I do it in my own way?"

LUCY CHING

Lucy Ching, blinded at age six months by a local rural herbalist in China, was born into a society that offered no training to the blind. Her struggle against heavy odds for a life and education illustrates a problem-solving method we can also use. When confronted by the impossible, our answer can become not "I can't" but "How do I do it in my own way?"

AFFIRMATION

There are answers to my difficulties; I will find them.

DAY 117

He who has a hundred miles to walk should reckon ninety as half the journey.

JAPANESE PROVERB
(QUOTED IN HERRIGE)

John Blofeld tells of being in rural China years ago talking with a Taoist monk in a lonely temple. The gruff monk asked Blofeld of his meditation practice. Blofeld, rather pleased with himself, gave some particular details. The monk was silent. Then he observed, "I'd say you're about seven eighths of the way there, you've got about seven out of eight of the principles of meditation." Then the monk gave a great laugh and added, "But the first seven don't count!"

These tasks where the results come only at the end are truly the difficult ones. Still, it can lighten our load to know their challenge and to find a few friends who follow our same paths.

AFFIRMATION

I accept difficult tasks with awareness.

DAY 118

If I had no sense of humor, I should long ago have committed suicide.
MAHATMA GANDHI
(QUOTED IN *QUOTATIONS TO CHEER YOU UP*)

Gandhi illustrates for us that no matter how life-shattering our problems and situations, we will be wise to encourage the knack of glancing at life through wry glasses. Laughing at ourselves is guaranteed to lighten the load. If Mahatma Gandhi can cultivate a sense of humor, so can we.

AFFIRMATION

Today I start a humor file; if I already have one, I add something to it.

DAY 119

Chaos records the birth of a new science. This new science offers a way of seeing order and pattern where formerly only the random, the erratic, the unpredictable—in short, the chaotic—had been observed. In the words of Douglas Hofstadter, "It turns out that an eerie type of chaos can lurk just behind a facade of order—and yet, deep inside the chaos lurks an even eerier type of order."
Although highly mathematical in origin, chaos is a science of the everyday world, addressing questions every child has wondered about: how clouds form, how smoke rises, how water eddies in a stream.
JAMES GLEICK, BACK COVER OF *CHAOS: MAKING A NEW SCIENCE*

AFFIRMATION

One way that I make order out of chaos is by always learning new things.

DAY 120

Synchronicity is not a phenomenon whose regularity it is at all easy to demonstrate. One is as much impressed by the disharmony of things as one is surprised by their occasional harmony. In contrast to the idea of a pre-established harmony, the synchronistic factor merely stipulates the existence of an intellectually necessary principle which could be added as a fourth to the recognized triad of space, time, and causality. These factors are necessary but not absolute.

C. G. JUNG

The factor of sychronicity has livened up my life considerably. And made it easier—which comes as a surprise to me. It's as if a new level of watcher is added, and in some real but quite subtle way, I am always noticing and adding and subtracting and coming to new conclusions and spaces. Like a spring migratory bird, I follow faint messages home—that is, to be where I'm supposed to be, with people I'm supposed to be with, doing what I'm supposed to be doing. In my mind's privacy, I describe this as turning off my mind! By which I mean, of course, my rational mind that believes only in heavy concrete objects with large captions on both front and back.

AFFIRMATION

I explore synchronicity to discover if it is a tool for me.

DAY 121

The world belongs to me because I understand it.

BALZAC
(QUOTED IN *THE ADVOCATE*)

"The one who understands more has more freedom—and more power," a friend says. "Once you understand something well enough you don't need to run from it," adds Robert Pirsig encouragingly in *Lila: An Inquiry Into Morals.*

Another friend says, "I'm learning the latest computer technology, and you'd better study too—if you don't want to end up old on the back roads of the information highway."

"I'm operating equipment that's over my head," I apologize to the laser printer technologist. He smiles, "That's all right we all are." A guilty weight drops from my shoulders as I realize I don't have to be perfect. Or run. My reasonable awareness and efforts will do just fine.

AFFIRMATION

I understand the technological needs of my world and I am not overwhelmed.

DAY 122

The most remarkable thing about Science is its youth. The earliest beginning of chemistry, as we now know it, certainly does not antedate Boyle's **Sceptical Chemist** *which appeared in 1661. . . . Archimedes discovered laws of physics around 250 B.C. but his discoveries hardly can be called the real beginning of physics. On the whole one is probably safe in saying that Science is less than 300 years old. This number has to be compared with the age of Humans, which is certainly greater than 100,000.* (Masculine nouns made generic.)

EUGENE P. WIGNER

AFFIRMATION

I refuse to be overawed by science or by those who use it as weapons.

Breaking the rules doesn't worry me anymore now that I can see that only one principle really matters. And that is rightness. . . . Establishments are no longer as stable as they used to be. They are having to make way for another kind of knowing which is concerned only with harmony, with keeping in touch with Earth's tune.

LYALL WATSON

In the wilds of the Amazon, Lyall Watson tells of his boatman's abscessed wisdom tooth. Watson tried to pull the tooth and couldn't. He agreed to visit a native healer rather than call off the trip. "He was a terrible man with little hair and fewer clothes. . . . Then the treatment began. Singing softly to himself in an Indian dialect, the healer . . . put his crooked forefinger into the mouth and stirred around in there. He . . . peered in again, and then reached in with thumb and forefinger and picked out the offending molar as though it had been simply lying there loose under the tongue."

But the healer wasn't finished; he still had to get rid of the pain. "I watched very closely, suddenly aware that this was not just a tired little man in rags, but a very impressive person. . . . What happened next brought a great roar of laughter from all the observers, but made the hair at the back of my neck bristle. Out of the side of [the patient's] mouth . . . came a column of live black army ants. . . . Ants marching two and three abreast, coming from somewhere and going somewhere."

The reason the native observers laughed was because their word for army ant and pain are the same and there went the pain marching out of his mouth. Lyall says it was years before he could bring himself to talk of the incident.

AFFIRMATION

As the Bard says, "There are more things in heaven and earth, Horatio, than are dreamt of in your philosophy."

DAY 124

A widespread misconception about mathematics is that it is completely hierarchical—first arithmetic, then algebra, then calculus, then more abstraction, then whatever. . . . This belief in the totem pole nature of mathematics isn't true, but it prevents many people who did poorly in seventh-grade, high school, or even college mathematics from picking up a popular book on the subject. Often very "advanced" mathematical ideas are more intuitive and comprehensible than are certain areas of elementary algebra.

JOHN ALLEN PAULOS

Taking a second look at what we've dismissed in our callow youth can be fun. Early on, I picked up John Steinbeck's *Tortilla Flat*, found his weird people distasteful, and so cheated myself of Steinbeck's fascinating characters and insightful mind. Fortunately for me, I later wised up enough to try again.

AFFIRMATION

With a soft heart, I take a new look at an old rejected area or topic.

DAY 125

Those who know others are clever;
Those who know themselves have discernment,
Those who overcome others have force;
Those who overcome themselves are strong.
Those who know contentment are rich;
Those who persevere are people of purpose.

PARAPHRASE OF LAO TZU

In a fast-paced culture where the superficial is king and the trivial masquerades as important, only the wise will make time to dive beneath the surface for richer meaning, to find heart and soul and to create balance in their lives.

AFFIRMATION

I have purpose, contentment, strength, and discernment.

DAY 126

It is extremely valuable to train the mind to stand apart and examine its own program. That, to me, is the definition of a liberal education—the ability to examine the programs of life against larger questions and purposes and other paradigms. Training, without such education, narrows and closes the mind so that the assumptions underlying the training are never examined. That's why it is so valuable to read broadly and to expose yourself to great minds.

STEPHEN R. COVEY

Keeping a journal is a wonderful tool for self-growth and self-training. Your journal is also a place where you can copy from great minds ideas that strike your fancy and that you want to remember and ponder. And perhaps to share and pass on to others.

AFFIRMATION

I regularly examine philosophies of life—my own and others.

DAY 127

Simply stated, people must believe that they are capable of solving a problem, of finding a new and better way. Or they won't. They can't if they don't believe in themselves, in their own capabilities. (No fair asking for new ideas in areas outside a co-worker's competence.)

TOM MELOHN

AFFIRMATION

I am a wonderful problem solver. And I'm good at helping other people too!

DAY 128

Paperwork simplification is defined as the organized application of common sense to eliminate waste and improve the productivity and effectiveness of paperwork. The organization is achieved by using techniques which enable people to see the work in ways they have not seen it before. The common sense is provided by those who have been doing the work.

BEN S. GRAHAM, JR.

It makes sense, doesn't it—that those who do the work should have clear input into the records and paperwork? Yet how tempting to add paperwork rather than take it away.

AFFIRMATION

My voice is on the side of less paperwork and bureaucracy.

DAY 129

Ask yourself what the real problem is, what constraints have to be met, and which ones can be changed or sacrificed . . . making thought concrete can help to cure confusion on nearly any occasion. When paths lead this way and that, circle back, and refuse to show the right way, make notes, make drawings, make models. Think aloud or form vivid mental images because such internal concreteness helps to clarify the problems.

A. DAVID SILVER

AFFIRMATION

I identify my problems in teaching and learning, in leading and living, and find solutions.

DAY 130

You can do whatever you want as long as you're willing to get up and do it.

REGINA BARRECA

This business of giving ourselves permission is complicated. Many of us exist encased (or imprisoned) within our beliefs. Suppose one morning we awake ready to do whatever we want. And we're willing to get up and begin those necessary large or small steps that will take us where we want to be.

AFFIRMATION

I examine an old dream in the light of new possibilities.

DAY 131

You have to know a lot about the old to see the new. Although one's education may be unconventional—and certainly in our own studies we have seen that creative individuals frequently reject the schools and teach themselves—it remains true that hard work and dedicated practice are the almost invariable precursors of original and distinctive achievement.

FRANK BARROW

AFFIRMATION

I foster hard work and dedicated practice.

DAY 132

How to Get More Breathing Space: Manage the beforehand. Create space for things in advance. Clear out the old and unsupportive and make room for what's ahead.

JEFF DAVIDSON

Jeff Davidson suggests we ask ourselves the obvious: What are we busy about? "Can we imagine," he asks, "Mahatma Gandhi or Martin Luther King getting up in the morning and lamenting about all the things they wanted to accomplish that day or week?"

AFFIRMATION

I sit down and decide what merits action and attention and what does not.

DAY 133

The further down life's road you go, the more you will learn that discipline, commitment and plain, old-fashioned guts come only to the person who works things through until they can stand at the mirror and say, "Well, it wasn't easy! But I like what I see looking back at me." (Masculine pronouns made generic.)

CHARLIE SHEDD

There's good news for us. Because we're living longer, we have more chances to get it right. In fact, Lydia Bronte says that half the people she interviewed for her book, *The Longevity Factor: The New Reality of Long Careers and How It Can Lead to Richer Lives*, started their period of peak creativity after age 50.

AFFIRMATION

I use my discipline, commitment, and stick-to-itiveness to find more and more ways to be creative.

DAY 134

Performances do not necessarily improve, even when you do them frequently. Indeed, it's common lore that people often end up practicing and entrenching their mistakes. . . . There's no reason why the right principles have to be as easy as a recipe for boiling water.

A. DAVID SILVER

As we all know, personal attention in teaching has no substitute. I once discovered my daughter in a gifted math class falling behind; she was adding in her head and then moving the abacus to show the answer!

Complexity is one of the high costs of our modern lives. To gain simplicity, we will have to earn it—probably by hard work.

AFFIRMATION

I am willing to do the work to clear up mistakes, to keep from making them, and to discover right principles.

DAY 135

I have found five steps that will help make service the centerpiece of leadership:

Focus on responsibilities
Emphasize values-based service
Make a commitment to personal service
Understand the needs of the people you wish to serve
Reconcile power with service

KESHAVAN NAIR

Keshavan Nair says that the service that Gandhi espoused was based on a moral imperative: You serve your fellow human being because it is the right thing to do. Nair adds that the rewards for such values-based service are personal fulfillment and a sense of satisfaction.

AFFIRMATION

I come to terms with the rewards I want from my work, and my life, understanding that these may change.

DAY 136

All successful entrepreneurs [and educators] have a unique ability to formulate problems. In economic terms, this means identifying a market or a problem in search of a solution. One of the compliments managers pay to entrepreneurs whom they join goes something like this: "She has the ability to see the whole market, from those customers who are ready to buy to those who need years of education."

A. DAVID SILVER

AFFIRMATION

I latch onto and use promising problem-solving methods and solutions from wherever I find them.

DAY 137

*You probably take for granted the many creative things you do every day. Planning a banquet, organizing a business event, designing a database, decorating a room, even choosing the clothes you wear are all endeavors that reward you with feelings of accomplishment. When you feel really good about something you have done, it is because you have done it creatively. **You have always been creative.***

NITA LELAND

AFFIRMATION

I frequently focus on the ways I am creative.

DAY 138

Six Roles of Teachers:

1. *The teacher as expert*
2. *The teacher as formal authority*
3. *The teacher as socializing agent*
4. *The teacher as facilitator*
5. *The teacher as ego ideal*
6. *The teacher as person*

WILBERT J. MCKEACHIE

What roles do you play? Which roles would you rather play? Sometimes it can be highly informative to simply list the tasks we perform and the roles we play.

AFFIRMATION

My roles and I are in harmony.

DAY 139

In twelve years at NATD, we learned that gains in quality—just like productivity—don't occur in quantum leaps. It's a little bit here, a little bit there, one day at a time. Perhaps we could liken quality gains at NATD to Ohio State's football offense under coach Woody Hayes: "Three yards and a cloud of dust; three yards and a cloud of dust." Nothing dramatic, certainly no sensational breakthroughs. Quality gains at NATD were the result of grinding it out every day and sticking to the basics. And the real taproot are the people: good people who care.

TOM MELOHN

Tom Melohn talks of values of honesty, trustworthiness, fairness, and mutual respect in his readable and intriguing book.

AFFIRMATION

I am a good person who cares about quality.

DAY 140

I was in second grade. We had weekly spelling tests and I had gotten 100 on all of them until one day in January. That day we had a substitute teacher. Since I was one of the tallest children in the class, I sat in the back of the room. We were doing the spelling tests. I never knew what I did that made her think I had cheated. But suddenly she came up behind me and with her red pencil wrote a huge "F" on my paper. I cried the rest of the day.

MEMORY OF SCHOOL
(QUOTED IN BLUMBERG AND BLUMBERG)

Some stories tell the whole story. Our actions both thoughtful and careless can have a vast impact.

AFFIRMATION

My actions are thoughtful.

DAY 141

He'd gotten temporarily sidetracked from his destiny.

JANET BURROWAY

That's the trouble with living a life that isn't over until it's over. (Also, most of us now have an extra 15 to 20 healthy years in middle age.) We never exactly know what's a detour from our destiny or what may be necessary experience. Sometimes when we finally see just how dead-ended a path is, we're too dispirited and tired to do much about it. In tough times I remind myself that change has to happen first in my mind. Then I look around for alternatives and get busy.

AFFIRMATION

My destiny makes me. I make my destiny.

DAY 142

A career is a patterned sequence of job-related experiences that span a person's life. First, the patterned sequence implies there is some order in the career planning process. Second, there is no mention of success or failure. Studies on the career management process make it clear there is no single process that constitutes a successful career. Third, the career span of most individuals includes a long period from the first job an individual holds to retirement. Fourth, a career includes attitudes that are feelings, thoughts, beliefs, and actions that individuals perform (accepting a job offer, quitting a job). Finally, a career consists of work-related experiences and any type of work performed (paid or unpaid) over a long period of time.

MARLENE K. STRADER AND PHILLIP J. DECKER

AFFIRMATION

I have a career plan. (Even if it does keep changing!) My career plan continues after normal retirement to include personal satisfaction.

DAY 143

A leader is a person you will follow to a place you wouldn't go by yourself.

JOEL ARTHUR BARKER

Joel Barker goes on to clear up a tricky point: the difference between visionaries and leaders. Visionaries have terrific ideas about the future, but no one is following the visionaries because they're all behind the leaders!

Warren Bennis adds in May 1990 in *Training* magazine (quoted in Barker) that the manager has his or her eye on the bottom line; the leader has her or his eye on the horizon.

AFFIRMATION

Vision and leadership, leaders and visionaries, all have their times and places in my life.

DAY 144

I was in the fifth grade. I was sitting next to this boy. I was kind of an intellectual snob and he really wasn't very smart. But one day I saw him drawing something that was really wonderful. I hadn't realized that he could do that and I knew that I couldn't do that. It really took me aback because it was my very first experience connected with school seeing somebody do something that I couldn't do. It stayed with me till this day. Kind of a bit of humility.

MEMORY OF SCHOOL
(QUOTED IN BLUMBERG AND BLUMBERG)

A friend once stunned me with the following definition. Humility: The recognition of one's own greatness.

AFFIRMATION

I ponder humility and its beneficial role in my life.

DAY 145

In our contemporary society, a typical day is loaded with stress; this may be the most stressful epoch in human history. . . . Repressed anger, depression, pessimism, egocentricity, shyness—all negative attitudes, all potential life shorteners. . . . The important thing is to learn how to deal with stress.

KATHY KEETON

Kathy Keeton again suggests diet, exercise, openness, and laughter to reduce stress, citing studies that show "laughter can be the equivalent of aerobic exercise (it accelerates the heart rate, improves blood circulation, and helps clear the breathing passages . . . while at the same time raising the levels of endorphins."

AFFIRMATION

I deal with stress in positive ways.

DAY 146

Again and again, Americans have espoused the merits of simple living, only to become enmeshed in its opposite. People have found it devilishly hard to limit their desires to their needs so as to devote most of their attention to "higher" activities. This should not surprise us. Socrates pointed out centuries ago that "many people will not be satisfied with the simpler way of life." . . . Thoreau likewise noted that simplicity was for the few rather than for the many. . . . Many Americans have not wanted to lead simple lives, and not wanting to is the best reason for not doing so.

DAVID E. SHI

AFFIRMATION

I live the life I want.

DAY 147

Vulgarity, blind conformity and mass lethargy need not triumph in the land of Lincoln and Frederick Douglass and Walt Whitman and Mark Twain. There is simply no reason why dreams should dry up like raisins or prunes or anything else in America. If you will permit me to say so, I believe that we can impose beauty on our future.

LORRAINE HANSBERRY

AFFIRMATION

I impose beauty on my future.
I help others impose beauty on their futures.

DAY 148

"Joe, I'm just a drummer. I've never been to college."
"Don't talk to me about college. I taught college. College is wonderful. Everyone who wants to should get to go, whenever they want to. But you don't have to go to college to become an educated man or woman."

JOSEPH CAMPBELL
(QUOTED IN HART)

When I was young and impressionable, I thought a Ph.D. guaranteed the acquisition of culture, including a certain modicum of morals, education, and intelligence. I know now that higher education may or may not guarantee "higher lives." And that good hearts, souls, and intelligence come in diverse forms and packages.

AFFIRMATION

I will continue my education for as long as I live.

DAY 149

Self-discipline without talent can often achieve astounding results, whereas talent without self-discipline inevitably dooms itself to failure.

SIDNEY HARRIS
(QUOTED IN LELAND)

An experimental attitude toward yourself can be quite useful. For example, when I was learning to write (that is, teaching myself how), I devised an experiment of (a) write when "inspired" and (b) sit down at the same time every day and stare for two hours at that blank piece of paper until something happens. After a couple of months (you can be somewhat casual about experiments on yourself), I looked at quality and quantity. Honesty forced me to admit (against my expectations) that quality for (a) and (b) was about the same. Ah, but quantity—here was a real difference. My self-imposed schedule helped me produce a lot more work. I've written on schedule ever since.

AFFIRMATION

I practice the self-discipline that will get me what I want.

DAY 150

We are using the power of lack of knowledge coupled with human creativity. The old rules maintained that you couldn't make a contribution until you knew enough. Wrong. You can make [a] significant contribution at any time.

JOEL ARTHUR BARKER

What a leap of faith we must make. And how scary and freeing is our new perspective. Yet somehow we knew it all along. The one who knows the most old facts is not necessarily the one who will make the new discoveries. Somehow, some way, the future has opened up (technology, so much knowledge is available, and our minds have opened) and extraordinary possibilities just hang there like ripe fruit on a tree.

Actually, of course, the fruit was always there. The difference is that now we know about fruit in new ways.

AFFIRMATION

I am inspired and inspiring.

DAY 151

Time Taxes. The earliest indicator of this paradigm shift has occurred in Littleton, Colorado. There, in 1990, a new program was born to lift the property tax burden off the elderly while gaining help for the schools.

The process is simple: Senior citizens go to the schools in the area and do various jobs. They help in the kitchen; they read to children in the classrooms; they monitor the bathrooms; they do calling to find out about absentees. In exchange, they are paid by having their property taxes reduced.

The results so far have been impressive.

JOEL ARTHUR BARKER

AFFIRMATION

I reach outside the lines for better ways to do things.

DAY 152

"But a teacher must be fair. That's the highest compliment a student pays a teacher . . . to say, 'she's fair.' No matter what: headaches, or worse. A teacher must be fair."

"Bullshit. No human being is fair all the time."

"A teacher isn't supposed to be human."

DOROTHY BRYANT

I know a woman who told her college classes (in the old days when 95% to 100% of the professors were male), "Watch me. This is how women teach! Or at least this one does."

Answer for yourself: Can teachers be both "fair" and human? Is there a higher value?

AFFIRMATION

I am an excellent educator.

DAY 153

Recently, I went to a center for teenage girls where the teacher asked what they would like to discuss most. Human biology? Care for their infant? Physiology of childbirth? Family planning? The girls showed no interest. Then the teacher asked, "Would you like to discuss how to say no to your boyfriend without losing his love?" All hands shot up.

EUNICE KENNEDY SHRIVER
(QUOTED IN LICKONA)

AFFIRMATION

I reach students and colleagues, friends and relatives, by reaching to where they are.

DAY 154

Chaucer wasn't preaching morality, so much as pointing out that you may as well make the very best of what you are sent, because, sure as hell, you aren't going to be sent anything else. One life is the ration. Nobody gets two Wednesdays.

JOAN AIKEN

I know someone who once impatiently told a whining client, "Look, it's simple. You either want to live or you don't. If you choose to live you might as well do the best you can. Take inventory. See where you are. And get on with it!" Or as Mary Ann Taylor-Hall says in *Come and Go, Molly Snow*:

> I float on my back on my breath. My heavy body, my space and time occupier, held up by breath on the surface, ten feet above the bottom of the pond. I choose not to drown. What do I choose instead? Breath. I choose to keep breathing, for forty or fifty more years.

AFFIRMATION

I make the best of what I have and I do what I can.

DAY 155

I remember as a kid being afraid of what was going to happen to me. The image of the musician as a kind of human meteorite who blazed briefly across the sky before burning up was strong during my childhood. Charlie Parker and Billie Holiday—these were heroes and warnings. I used to wonder what it was about this need that had chosen me that it could make a grown man give up everything, even to the point of relinquishing life, to achieve what was usually the briefest of connections. Sometimes I felt that I was running as fast as I could with a blindfold on.

MICKEY HART

AFFIRMATION

I honor talent and genius in myself and in others, especially children and young adults.

DAY 156

Once in seven years I burn all my sermons: for it is a shame if I cannot write better sermons now than I did seven years ago.

JOHN WESLEY, JOURNAL, SEPTEMBER 1, 1778
(QUOTED IN ROEN)

We've all known people who cling to the past like glue for whatever reason. And we've seen the trouble this gets them into. Could these people also be us?

AFFIRMATION

I easily make the effort to keep myself up to date.

DAY 157

Yes, children do grow up entirely too fast. They start out just babes in arms, but before you know it, you've turned around and they're gone . . . and usually it's with your car!

MARTHA BOLTON

And oh what a mistake we make if we think those little creatures will always be grateful—perhaps, on their way, to take a moment to say, "Thank you for your help and sacrifices; you've been wonderful!" It may happen, but we can't count on it. We truly do have to be magnificent and take care of ourselves. To be careful and not make one-sided bargains like so many mothers do: I'll give extra now and later they'll appreciate it. The child, rightfully, has no part of the mother's bargain. Those we teach and who are under our care have no part of our bargains. It's up to us to know and accept what we're doing—along with its possible consequences.

AFFIRMATION

I take care of myself and give what I give with no strings attached.

DAY 158

The only things that can be taught are barely worth teaching, and the things most worth teaching can't be taught. (Masculine nouns made generic.)

PETER KREEFT

What do you think of the above quote? How about the following from page 11 of this same resource: "Really to ask a question is harder than to answer it, for once the question is asked with all the passion of your being, it will be answered. All real seekers find. The universe is a great Answer [Machine], but it answers only questioners."

AFFIRMATION

I ask myself and the universe the right questions.
I allow myself to hear the right answers.

DAY 159

Once upon a time there was a woman who was just like all women. And she married a man who was just like all men. And they had some children who were just like all children. And it rained all day. . . .
The woman read love stories and longed for things to be different.
The children fought and yelled and played and had scabs on their knees.
In the end they all died.

ELIZABETH SMART

Elisabeth Kubler-Ross reminds us that when we die, we may not have time to do all we've planned. Better do it now!

AFFIRMATION

I am doing what I want to do, living as I want to live.

DAY 160

When I started teaching, it seemed to me we had the support of maybe 80 percent of the parents. Then each year it kept declining until it was about half and half, and then it seemed as if it was maybe 80-20 against teachers. But in the last few years I've seen a change, until now I think we're getting the support of most parents again.

Sometimes you feel like a very small influence as a teacher, shoveling against the tide. But then you find out there are more people like you than you realize, people who share your values. They're out there.

RON WOODS
(QUOTED IN LICKONA)

AFFIRMATION

I look beyond the immediate to discover the enduring.

DAY 161

Some things lead and some follow;
Some breathe gently and some breathe hard;
Some are strong and some are weak;
Some destroy and some are destroyed.
. . . The sage avoids excess, extravagance, and arrogance.

LAO TZU

Every so often I ask myself if I am shouting against the wind. Sam Reifler's *I Ching* says that the person who arrogantly shouts commands into the wind is acting absurdly—like King Lear, they are mad. "To be without humility toward other [people] is misguided and egotistical; to be without humility toward heaven is purely and simply derangement."

AFFIRMATION

My efforts and energy are realistically focused.

DAY 162

Respectability is of course a public attitude: it has nothing to do with private conduct—this has always been so. It has only to do with witnessed behavior, nothing with what we do in private. Call it discretion, if you will; respectability is based in discretion and discretion has deception at its core. Hypocrisy is built into the respectable life. But denying the headmistress of a school, and precisely on the ground of her maturity, the sexual freedom that's given the students in her charge goes beyond hypocrisy to say with some firmness that sex is only for the young.

DIANA TRILLING

Trilling calls Dr. Tarnower's home "a mean household" and says, "The eminent physician wasn't a very bright man; selfishness like his makes a person stupid."

To me, Jean Harris failed to keep her priorities straight, to name to herself exactly what she was doing (if she chose to do it) and to be willing to pay the price. This is surely a major reason for marriage: that obligations to each other will be formalized, roles spelled out, and rules made for contingencies.

Whatever her faults and her tragedy, Jean Harris has my sympathy; Tarnower never did.

AFFIRMATION

I am comfortable with my discretion and with my public face.

DAY 163

Wyn realized she was alone on the terrace with a sextet of sere winter women, readying themselves to go into the cafe. She wondered if, down the line, she wouldn't become a winter woman: manless, childless, self-sufficient because she had to be, wringing what cheer she could out of sisterly affection and the Annual Literary Arts Symposium.

It was a destiny difficult for some to escape and Wyn wasn't even certain she wanted to. There was a great deal of comfort to be found among one's own kind in one's own place.

DAVID A. KAUFELT

AFFIRMATION

I look for support and comfort where I can find them.
I create support and comfort for myself. And for others.

DAY 164

The beginning of the path to peace is the end of life unlived. It is a finishing of unfinished business. To finish business means an end of relationships as business. It is not a totalling of accounts. It is not a waiting for another's acceptance or forgiveness. It is an acceptance of them and ourselves, as is. Even if that "as is" includes their not accepting us. When we have touched another with forgiveness we no longer require anything in return. Our business is done.

STEPHEN LEVINE

Not requiring anything in return is key, I believe. As long as we still want others to know how wonderful we are, how much we sacrificed for them, or even how much we love them (if we're requiring something in return), then we remain bound to the old situation.

Our road to freedom is to forgive, to let go and to move on to a chosen life that suits us better. (If you know someone who's hung up on forgiveness, Levine's article contains an excellent "Guided Forgiveness Meditation.")

AFFIRMATION

I open my heart for forgiveness and for letting go.

DAY 165

When Laurel looked at Walter Wheeler, it struck her that people are as immovable as rock. The force it takes to move them leaves them scarred; as many end up rubble as learn how to build.

JANET BURROWAY

Frequently, we're aware of exactly what changes, in ourselves and in others, need to be made. Yet bringing about that change can be astonishingly difficult. Allen Wheelis's small oldie but goodie, *How People Change*, is an encouraging book on the topic.

AFFIRMATION

I foster the changes I want in myself and in others.

DAY 166

We don't stop laughing because we grow old; we grow old because we stop laughing.

ANONYMOUS
(QUOTED IN QUOTATIONS TO CHEER YOU UP)

Once, when I knew laughter was going out of my life and depression would be raining in, I made a list of all the things that made me feel good: taking a bath, visiting the library, hot chocolate on a cool afternoon, and so on.

The bad news is, I lost my list. The better news is, the anticipated depression never arrived. Without planning, I'd incorporated my list into my daily life and was busy enjoying life. (There's help for clinical depression; if you need it, you should seek it.)

AFFIRMATION

Today, just for fun, I make a list of ten nice things I can do for myself—smiling all the while. Then I do one.

At a very simple level, ritual allays anxiety. It can resolve tension by focusing attention on some positive and trusted action. When Gunung Api [the volcano] begins to make ominous rumbling sounds, there are only three things you can do. You can ignore it: you can rush to the mosque and pray for deliverance; or you can work magic through the performance of an established rite. Prayer helps, but it is no more than a request. It could be refused or ignored. It is certainly more smoothing than doing nothing, but magic is the most comforting of all. Magic is guaranteed as long as you get the ritual right. Everything depends on you.

At the very least, ritual changes those who take part.

LYALL WATSON

Claude Steiner in *Scripts People Live* finds that people can structure their time together in one of six ways: withdrawal, ritual, pastimes (golf, bridge, tennis), games (as in *Games People Play* by Eric Berne), work, and intimacy. When I was younger, I was determined to concentrate on work and intimacy. But now I find that ritual soothes my emotions and connects me to my past and future.

AFFIRMATION

I attend to my rituals, learning to take pleasure in them.

DAY 168

There are two kinds of strength. One brings out the strength of the other, helps it to be born: the other kind imposes its own strength and weakens those who submit to it.

ANAÏS NIN

When we teach others by our behavior (or lack of it) that they can act irresponsibly, we create monsters. We will pick up their crayons, do their homework, accept their ill-temper, pay their fees, give one more last 99th chance to the undeserving.

Now is the time to kill off the monstrous behaviors we have fostered—including those inside us.

AFFIRMATION

I don't allow others to take advantage of my strengths.
I discover and help develop my student's strengths.

DAY 169

She wondered how many papers she must have read and marked through the years. Forty years. Two hundred students each semester. One paper each week from each student. Thirty-eight teaching weeks in each year. Two hundred times thirty-eight times forty . . . papers, stacks, miles high, toppling, sagging, crushed, and covered with words, words, an avalanche of scrawled words on tons of paper, coming at me, no, not an avalanche, a tidal wave, growing, rising as it moves on me, coming to bury . . .

DOROTHY BRYANT

Yes, sometimes teaching is monotonous and a tiresome drudgery. Still, I aim my mind and behavior for the principles of good education.

AFFIRMATION

My teaching and learning are always improving.

DAY 170

I've been a hard worker all my life, . . . but 'most all my work has been the kind that "perishes with the using," as the Bible says. That's the discouragin' thing about a woman's work. Milly Amos used to say that if a woman was to see all the dishes that she had to wash before she died, piled up before her in one pile, she'd lie down and die right then and there. . . . But when one of my grandchildren or great-grandchildren sees one o' these quilts, they'll think about Aunt Jane, and, wherever I am then, I'll know I ain't forgotten.

I reckon everybody wants to leave somethin' behind that'll last after they're dead and gone.

ELIZA CALVERT HALL
(QUOTED IN SEWELL)

AFFIRMATION

I know what I'll leave behind and I'm preparing.

DAY 171

What if you try harder and it doesn't help? What if you see that the failure's not your fault, but you're still the one who's failed?

DANIEL PETERS

As the song says, nobody has ever promised us that all our gardens will always be filled with yellow roses. The spiritual solution, I tell myself, is always possible—I can learn from my mistakes and failures.

AFFIRMATION

I forgive myself for necessary failure.
I grieve and move on.

DAY 172

Whenever I feel myself inferior to everything about me, threatened by my own mediocrity, frightened by the discovery that a muscle is losing its strength, a desire its power, or a pain the keen edge of its bite, I can still hold up my head and say to myself, . . . "I am the daughter of a woman who, in a mean, close-fisted, confined little place, opened her village home to stray cats, tramps, and pregnant servant girls. I am the daughter of a woman . . . who herself never ceased to flower, untiringly, during three quarters of a century.

COLETTE
(QUOTED IN OLSEN)

AFFIRMATION

I never cease to flower.
I never cease to help others to flower.

DAY 173

Some people say there is a new sun every day, that it begins its life at dawn and lives for one day only.
    They say you have to welcome it.

BYRD BAYLOR

When is the last time you gave yourself a day—for mental health, for healing, for rejuvenation, for goals, for the relaxation of piddling around, for joy?

AFFIRMATION

I welcome each day.

DAY 174

*God's ways are mysterious. There are instances in which humans con-
fronted with an act of God, reel back in horror and disgust at the wanton
destruction, the cruelty, the violence, the pointlessness of it all. If Friends
have one message to give the world, it is this: It is not up to God to justify
the apparent senselessness of some of his most shocking acts. It is up to us,
individual men and women, to relieve our brother's or sister's cruel fate of
its apparent pointlessness by turning it into a beacon that will shine
through the ages.* (Masculine nouns made generic.)

JAN DE HARTOG

AFFIRMATION

*In my own way, I change
Experience into awareness,
Awareness into wisdom, and
Wisdom into action, remembering
No action is sometimes the strongest action of all.*

DAY 175

*When Gandhi left the scene of political power in 1946 to visit the riot-torn
areas of India, he was seventy-seven years old. His schedule was brutal. He
worked fifteen to eighteen hours a day and walked 116 miles in sixty days
to comfort victims in forty-six villages. Here, in the midst of unspeakable
savagery, was a frail individual with the courage to fulfill his commitment
to truth and nonviolence. He asked those who had suffered to forgive, and,
at the same time, asked those who perpetuated the violence to repent.*

KESHAVAN NAIR

AFFIRMATION

I study great lives and become a better person.

DAY 176

It was what you were, rather than any specific thing you taught me, that became a standard for me. What a teacher is can't be hidden or faked; it is there, day by day, in that intimate and intense contact of daily class work. There were days when you were tired, days when you were frustrated, days when the students who were unready (and might always be) to accept what you offered, must have been unbearable. There was your personal life, of which we knew nothing, but which could not have been easier than that of most people.

But you were the same every day: strict, demanding, impartial and fair. You were as certain as the sun rising each day. And, I suppose, most students thought of you as a natural phenomenon rather than as a human being. No young person knows what it costs to be so egoless, to remain consistent, no matter what the pressures. We only learn this by growing older, if we ever learn it. Whether or not we ever do learn it depends a great deal, I think, on the memory of successful examples, which encourage us as we try and fail and try again.

In impossible conditions you fought to do your work.

DOROTHY BRYANT

This is part of a letter to "Miss Giardino" from a former student.

AFFIRMATION

To the best of my ability, I do my work.

DAY 177

"And how long do you think we can keep up this goddamn coming and going?" he asked.

Florentino Ariza had kept his answer ready for fifty-three years, seven months, and eleven days and nights.

"Forever," he said.

GABRIEL GARCIA MARQUEZ

And how long do you think you can keep doing what you're doing?

Sometimes—when we've got it right—the right answer really is "Forever."

AFFIRMATION

I have things that I can do forever.

DAY 178

And so the sun will pass away—die away. Tones of blue—of deep quiet— lively blue—float down and all the people's voices seem to grow quiet— quiet.

And I remember all the twilights I have ever known—they float across my eyes.

I think of forests and picnics—of being very warm in something cotton. Of smelling earth—and loving life.

Long live good life! And beauty . . . and love!

LORRAINE HANSBERRY

Lorraine Hansberry died at the age of 34 of cancer. In 1959, she became the youngest American playwright, the fifth woman, and the only Black writer ever to win the New York Drama Critics Circle award for the Best Play of the Year.

AFFIRMATION

I love my life and my world.

DAY 179

'Twas grace that taught my heart to fear
And grace my fears relieved
How precious did that grace appear
The hour I first believed.

Through many dangers, toils and snares
We have already come
'Twas grace that brought us safe thus far
And grace will lead us home.

MIDDLE TWO VERSES OF AMAZING GRACE, JOHN NEWTON
SONG WRITTEN BEFORE THE CIVIL WAR

AFFIRMATION

I do what I can. My heart is happy.

DAY 180

To retire when the task is accomplished
Is the way of heaven.

LAO TZU

Retiring when the task is completed seems the exact opposite of the Peter Principle of being promoted to the level of our incompetence. In other words, we do a good job where we are and so of course "earn" a promotion—to a level where we may be incompetent and unhappy. (It's also important to remember that just because we can do something doesn't mean we like doing it.) We can also "self-promote" ourselves to unsuitable tasks where we continue flailing away simply because we hate to give up.

Sometimes we even do tasks without naming them to ourselves—so how can we know when they are completed?

AFFIRMATION

I know when a task is accomplished and I retire if it is appropriate.

READING LIST

The following is a short list of highly prized, helpful books. A complete reference list follows.

Joel Arthur Barker, *Paradigms: The Business of Discovering the Future* (New York: Harper Business, 1992).

Lee G. Bolman and Terrence E. Deal, *Leading With Soul: An Uncommon Journey of Spirit* (San Francisco: Jossey-Bass, 1995).

Dorothy Bryant, *Miss Giardino* (Berkeley, CA: Ata Books, 1978).

Melodie Chenevert, *STAT: Special Techniques in Assertiveness Training* (St. Louis, MO: C. V. Mosby Company, 1983).

Max De Pree, *Leadership Is an Art* (New York: Dell Trade Paperback, 1989).

Carl Hammerschlag, *The Dancing Healers: A Journey to Spiritual Healing With Native Americans* (New York: Simon & Schuster, 1993).

Lorraine Hansberry, *To Be Young, Gifted and Black* (New York: Signet, 1970).

James W. Jones, *In the Middle of This Road We Call Our Life: The Courage to Search for Something More* (San Francisco: Harper, 1995).

Thomas Lickona, *Educating for Character: How Our Schools Can Teach Respect and Responsibility* (New York: Bantam Books, 1991).

Tom Melohn, *The New Partnership: Profit by Bringing Out the Best in Your People, Customers, and Yourself* (Essex Junction, VT: Oliver Wight Publications, 1994).

Maureen Murdock, *The Heroine's Journey: Woman's Quest for Wholeness* (Boston: Shambhala, 1990).

Keshavan Nair, *A Higher Standard of Leadership: Lessons From the Life of Gandhi* (San Francisco: Berrett-Koehler, 1994).

Anne Wilson Schaef, *Women's Reality: An Emerging Female System in a White Male Society* (New York: HarperCollins, 1981).

Marilyn Sewell, Ed., *Cries of the Spirit: A Celebration of Women's Spirituality* (Boston: Beacon Press, 1991).

Barbara Sher, *Wishcraft: How to Get What You Really Want* (New York: Ballantine Books, 1979).

Claude M. Steiner, *Scripts People Live: Transactional Analysis of Life Scripts* (New York: Bantam Books, 1974).

Kenneth G. Wilson, *Redesigning Education* (New York: Holt, 1994).

REFERENCES

The Advocate, December 1994.

Joan Aiken, *Background* (New York: Doubleday, 1989).

Sherry Anderson and Patricia Hopkins, *The Feminine Face of God* (New York: Bantam Books, 1991).

Margaret Atwood, *The Robber Bride* (New York: Bantam Books, 1993).

Joel Arthur Barker, *Paradigms: The Business of Discovering the Future* (New York: Harper Business, 1992).

Regina Barreca, *Perfect Husbands (& Other Fairy Tales)* (New York: Harmony Books, 1993).

Regina Barreca, *They Used to Call Me Snow White . . . But I Drifted: Women's Strategic Use of Humor* (New York: Viking, 1991).

Frank Barrow, *Creative Person and Creative Process* (New York: Holt, Rinehart & Winston, 1969).

Byrd Baylor, *The Way to Start a Day* (New York: Macmillan Publishing, 1986).

Eric Berne, *Games People Play* (New York: Ballantine Books, 1985).

Arthur Blumberg and Phyllis Blumberg, *The Unwritten Curriculum: Things Learned But Not Taught in School* (Thousand Oaks, CA: Corwin Press, 1994).

Lee G. Bolman and Terrence E. Deal, *Leading With Soul: An Uncommon Journey of Spirit* (San Francisco: Jossey-Bass, 1995).

Martha Bolton, "Martha's Laugh Lines," *The Pen Woman*, September 1986.

Martha Bolton, "Martha's Laugh Lines," *The Pen Woman*, October-November 1986.

Lydia Bronte, *The Longevity Factor: The New Reality of Long Careers and How It Can Lead to Richer Lives* (New York: HarperCollins, 1993).

Dorothy Bryant, *Miss Giardino* (Berkeley, CA: Ata Books, 1978).

James Lee Burke, *A Stained White Radiance* (New York: Hyperion, 1992).

Janet Burroway, *Cutting Stone* (Boston: Houghton Mifflin, 1992).

A. Camus, *The Fall* (New York: Vintage Books, 1956).

Melodie Chenevert, *STAT: Special Techniques in Assertiveness Training* (St. Louis, MO: C. V. Mosby Company, 1983).

Lucy Ching, *One of the Lucky Ones* (London: Shere Books Ltd., 1980).

Robert Coles, *Children of Crisis* (New York: Dell Publishing, 1964).

Stephen R. Covey, *The 7 Habits of Highly Effective People: Restoring the Character Ethic* (New York: Simon & Schuster, 1989).

Mihaly Csikszentmihalyi, *Flow: The Psychology of Optimal Experience* (New York: HarperPerennial, 1990).

Dolores Curran, *Traits of a Healthy Family* (Minneapolis, MN: Winston Press, 1983).

Mary Daheim, *Holy Terrors* (New York: Avon Books, 1992).

Jeff Davidson, *Breathing Space: Living & Working at a Comfortable Pace in a Sped-Up Society* (New York: MasterMedia, 1991).

Jan De Hartog, *The Peculiar People* (New York: Pantheon Books, 1992).

Max De Pree, *Leadership Is an Art* (New York: Dell Trade Paperback, 1989).

Charles Dickens, *A Christmas Carol* (New York: Pocket Books, 1939).

Earthworks Group, *50 Simple Things You Can Do to Save the Earth* (Berkeley, CA: Earthworks Press, 1989).

Riane Eisler, *The Chalice and the Blade: Our History, Our Future* (San Francisco: Harper & Row, 1987).

Herbert Fingarette, *Self-Deception* (London: Routledge & Kegan Paul, 1969).

Nicholas Freeling, *Love in Amsterdam* (New York: Penguin Books, 1962).

Kinky Friedman, *Frequent Flyer* (New York: Berkley Publishing Group, 1989).

Marilyn Galtin, *When I Listen* (Santa Fe, NM: Ocean Tree Books, 1985).

Haim Ginott, *Teacher and Child* (New York: Avon Books, 1976).

James Gleick, *Chaos: Making a New Science* (New York: Penguin Books, 1988).

Ben S. Graham, Jr., "Paperwork Simplification." In Robert N. Lehrer, Ed., *White Collar Productivity* (New York: McGraw-Hill, 1983).

Carl A. Hammerschlag, *The Theft of the Spirit* (New York: Simon & Schuster, 1994).

Lorraine Hansberry, *To Be Young, Gifted and Black* (New York: Signet, 1970).

Mickey Hart, *Drumming at the Edge of Magic* (San Francisco: Harper, 1990).

Eugen Herrige, *Zen in the Art of Archery* (New York: Vintage Books, 1971).

Kathryn B. Johnson, *Attitude Adjustment* (Key Biscayne, FL: Attitude Adjustment, 1993).

James W. Jones, *In the Middle of This Road We Call Our Life* (San Francisco: Harper, 1995).

C. S. Jung, *Synchronicity,* translated by R.F.C. Hull (Princeton, NJ: Princeton University Press, 1960).

David A. Kaufelt, *The Winter Women Murders* (New York: Pocket Books, 1994).

Kathy Keeton, *Longevity: The Science of Staying Young* (New York: Viking, 1992).

Cheris Kramarae and Paula A. Treichler, *A Feminist Dictionary* (San Francisco: Thorsons, 1992).

Peter Kreeft, *A Turn of the Clock: A Book of Modern Proverbs* (San Francisco: Ignatius Press, 1987).

Elisabeth Kubler-Ross, *Death: The Final Stage of Growth* (Englewood Cliffs, NJ: Prentice-Hall, 1975).

Natalie Kusz, *Road Song* (New York: HarperCollins, 1991).

Lao Tzu, *Tao Te Ching* (New York: Penguin Classics, 1963).

Joan Mathews Larson, *Seven Weeks to Sobriety: The Proven Program to Fight Alcoholism Through Nutrition* (New York: Fawcett Columbine, 1992).

Nita Leland, *The Creative Artist: A Fine Artist's Guide to Expanding Your Creativity and Achieving Your Artistic Potential* (Cincinnati, OH: North Light Books, 1990).

Katharine Le Meé, *Chant: The Origins, Form, Practice, and Healing Power of Gregorian Chant* (New York: Bell Tower, 1994).

Stephen Levine, "Forgiveness," *The Quest,* Summer 1992.

Thomas Lickona, *Educating for Character: How Our Schools Can Teach Respect and Responsibility* (New York: Bantam Books, 1991).

Jo Ann Lordahl, *Money Meditations for Women* (Berkeley, CA: Celestial Arts, 1994).

Thomas Mann, in *Bartlett's Familiar Quotations* (Boston: Little, Brown, 1951).

Gabriel Garcia Marquez, *Love in the Time of Cholera* (New York: Penguin Books, 1985).

Gerald May, *Addiction and Grace* (San Francisco: Harper, 1991).

Wilbert J. McKeachie, *Teaching Tips: A Guide Book for the Beginning College Teacher,* 7th ed. (Lexington, MA: D. C. Heath, 1978).

Tom Melohn, *The New Partnership: Profit by Bringing Out the Best in Your People, Customers, and Yourself* (Essex Junction, VT: Oliver Wight Publications, 1994).

Deng Ming-Dao, *365 Tao: Daily Meditations* (San Francisco: Harper, 1992).

Marlo Morgan, *Mutant Message* (New York: HarperCollins, 1991).

David M. Moriarty, *Psychic Energy* (Springfield, IL: Charles C Thomas, 1964).

Mark Morrison-Reed and Jacqui James, Eds., *Been in the Storm So Long: A Meditation Manual* (Boston: Skinner Books, 1991).

Maureen Murdock, *The Heroine's Journey: Woman's Quest for Wholeness* (Boston: Shambhala, 1990).

Keshavan Nair, *A Higher Standard of Leadership: Lessons From the Life of Gandhi* (San Francisco: Berrett-Koehler, 1994).

Helen and Scott Nearing, *Living the Good Life: How to Live Sanely and Simply in a Troubled World* (New York: Galahad Books, 1954).

Anaïs Nin, *Diaries of Anaïs Nin,* Vols. 1-7 (New York: Harcourt Brace Jovanovich, 1966-1980).

Tillie Olsen, *Mother to Daughter, Daughter to Mother* (Old Westbury, NY: Feminist Press, 1984).

José Ortega y Gasset, *The Revolt of the Masses* (New York: Norton, 1932).

John Allen Paulos, *Beyond Numeracy* (New York: Knopf, 1991).

M. Scott Peck, *The Road Less Traveled* (Simon & Schuster, 1988).

Anne Perry, *A Dangerous Mourning* (New York: Fawcett Columbine, 1991).

Laurence J. Peter, *The Peter Principle* (New York: Bantam Books, 1969).

Daniel Peters, *Rising in the Ruins* (New York: Random House, 1995).

William Pickens with William L. Andrews, Ed., *Bursting Bonds: The Autobiography of a "New Negro"* (Bloomington: Indiana University Press, 1991).

Marge Piercy, "To Be of Use," *Circles on the Water* (1982). Quoted in Rosalie Maggio, Ed., *The Beacon Book of Quotations by Women* (Boston: Beacon Press, 1992).

Robert M. Pirsig, *Lila: An Inquiry Into Morals* (New York: Bantam Books, 1991).

Connie Podesta, *Self-Esteem and the Six-Second Secret* (Newbury Park, CA: Corwin Press, 1990).

Richard R. Powell, Stanley J. Zehm, and Jeffrey A. Kottler, *Classrooms Under the Influence: Addicted Families/Addicted Students* (Thousand Oaks, CA: Corwin Press, 1995).

Quotations to Cheer You Up (New York: Wings Books, 1991).

Ayn Rand, *Atlas Shrugged* (New York: Random House, 1957).

David Reich, "Fighting the Right on Abortion Clinic Access," *The World,* January-February 1995.

Sam Reifler, *I Ching: A New Interpretation for Modern Times* (New York: Bantam Books, 1985).

Rainer Maria Rilke, *Letters to a Young Poet* (Boston: Shambhala, 1993).

William H. Roen, *The Inward Ear* (New York: Albany Institute, 1989).

Elisabeth Ruedy and Sue Nirenberg, *Where Do I Put the Decimal Point? How to Conquer Math Anxiety and Increase Your Facility With Numbers* (New York: Henry Holt, 1990).

Anne Wilson Schaef, *Women's Reality: An Emerging Female System in a White Male Society* (New York: HarperCollins, 1981).

George Seldes (compiled by), *The Great Thoughts* (New York: Ballantine Books, 1985).

Marilyn Sewell, Ed., *Cries of the Spirit: A Celebration of Women's Spirituality* (Boston: Beacon Press, 1991).

Charlie Shedd, *Letters to Philip* (New York: Doubleday, 1968).

Barbara Sher, *Wishcraft: How to Get What You Really Want* (New York: Ballantine Books, 1979).

David E. Shi, *The Simple Life: Plain Living and High Thinking in American Culture* (New York: Oxford University Press, 1985).

A. David Silver, *Enterprising Woman: Lessons From 100 of the Greatest Entrepreneurs of Our Day* (New York: AMACOM, 1994).

Marsha Sinetar, *A Way Without Words: A Guide for Spiritually Emerging Adults* (Mahwah, NJ: Paulist Press, 1992).

Elizabeth Smart, *By Grand Central Station I Sat Down and Wept* (New York: Vintage International, 1966, 1992).

Lewis B. Smedes, *Choices: Making the Decisions in a Complex World* (San Francisco: Harper, 1991).

John Steinbeck, *Sea of Cortez* (Mararoneck, NY: P. P. Appel, 1971).

Claude M. Steiner, *Scripts People Live: Transactional Analysis of Life Scripts* (New York: Bantam Books, 1974).

Autumn Stephens, *Wild Women: Crusaders, Curmudgeons and Completely Corsetless Ladies in the Otherwise Virtuous Victorian Era* (Emeryville, CA: Conari Press, 1992).

John Stoltenberg, "Other Men." Quoted in Franklin Abbott, Ed., *New Men, New Minds* (Freedom, CA: Crossing Press, 1987).

Marlene K. Strader and Phillip J. Decker, *Role Transition: To Patient Care Management* (Norwalk, CT: Appleton & Lange, 1995).

Mary Ann Taylor-Hall, *Come and Go, Molly Snow* (New York: Norton, 1995).

Diana Trilling, *Mrs. Harris: The Death of the Scarsdale Diet Doctor* (New York: Harcourt Brace, 1981).

Mark Twain, *Pudd'nhead Wilson* (New York: NAL-Dutton, 1964).

Herbert F. Vetter, Ed., *Speak Out Against the New Right* (Boston: Beacon Press, 1982).

Aubury Wallace, *Green Means: Living Gently on the Planet* (San Francisco: KQED Books, 1994).

Lyall Watson, *Gifts of Unknown Things* (New York: Simon & Schuster, 1976).

Allen Wheelis, *How People Change* (New York: Harper & Row, 1970).

Gail White, "The Escapee," in *Calyx: A Journal of Art & Literature by Women*, Winter 1994-1995, No. 3.

Eugene P. Wigner, "The Limits of Science." In Herbert Feigl and May Brodbeck, Eds., *Readings in the Philosophy of Science* (New York: Appleton-Century-Crofts, 1953).

Kenneth G. Wilson, *Redesigning Education* (New York: Holt, 1994).

Wabun Wind, *Women of the Dawn* (New York: Berkley Publishing Group, 1991).

Lyric Wallwork Winik, "We Are Responsible," *Parade Magazine,* March 19, 1995.

CORWIN
PRESS

The Corwin Press logo—a raven striding across an open book—represents the happy union of courage and learning. We are a professional-level publisher of books and journals for K–12 educators, and we are committed to creating and providing resources that embody these qualities. Corwin's motto is "Success for All Learners."